Contents

Volume 100:1 Spring 2010

EDITORIAL

FIONA SAMPSON

I t's a myth, of course, that poets are apolitical, though tone-deaf commentators may hear only polemic as politically engaged. Poetry speaks as it finds, and what it finds is, in many cases, an acute awareness of the world around us – in all its disappearing complexity.

So this issue is full of glimpses of the natural world. It's also full of encounters with world culture: from Iceland, Mexico and Denmark to Australia and America. These are the worlds – natural and human – within which today's British poetry finds itself. But British poetry has also just been through its annual prize-giving season. Like druids brightening a solstice with sacrifices, its seems, we choose the winter months for these ceremonies. While the new Eliot prize-winner, Philip Gross, is reviewed here, and *PR* was the only magazine (apart from Areté, his publisher) to bring you a preview of Christopher Reid's Costa-prize-winning *A Scattering*, this issue also both celebrates our own Geoffrey Dearmer prize and publishes the Poetry Society's National Poetry Competition winners. In addition to prizewinners Helen Dunmore, Ian Pindar and John Stammers, whose poems are featured on pp. 86-88, NPC judges Daljit Nagra, Ruth Padel and Neil Rollinson, picked twelve runners-up: Julie Collar, Peter Kahn, Valerie Laws, Neil Lockwood, J.P. Nosbaum, Frank Ortega, Sam Riviere, Cherry Smyth, Jon Stone and Jane Yeh. Elsewhere, Glyn Maxwell picked Maitreyabandhu's 'The Visitation' as the winner of the Geoffrey Dearmer Prize for this year's best poem in the Review by a poet yet to publish a book.

Maitreyabandhu's work beautifully, and seriously, contains the possibilities which other traditions might call insight: and in doing so it returns us to the continuing, year-round business of poetry, beyond the hustle and din of competition, which is, perhaps, to cultivate awareness – among other things, of *Our Disappearing World*.

CONTRIBUTORS

The National Poetry Competition winners are Helen Dunmore, Ian Pindar and John Stammers. *Helen Dunmore's latest novel,* The Betrayal, *is due in April. Ian Pindar's first collection* Emporium *appears from Carcanet in 2011, and his second the year after. John Stammers's next collection,* Interior Night, *is published by Picador in April.*

Liz Berry has an Eric Gregory Award. *The Patron Saint of Schoolgirls* is forthcoming (tall-lighthouse, May). **Arthur Boyars** appeared in *The New Poetry*. **David Briggs**'s first collection is *The Method Men* (Salt). **Dan Burt**'s *Searched for Text* is forthcoming from Carcanet. **Lynn Foote**'s pamphlet is due from Hearing Eye. **Leah Fritz** has published three collections. **Tom Gilliver** is reading English at Christ's, Cambridge. **John Greening** received a Cholmondeley Award in 2008. **David Grubb**'s next collection is *The Man Who Talked to Owls* (Shearsman, May). **James Harpur**'s *The Dark Age* (Anvil) won the 2009 Michael Hartnett Award. **Paul Henry**'s *The Brittle Sea – New & Selected Poems* is out from Seren this autumn. **Jane Hirshfield** won the Poetry Center Book Award. **Paul Hodgson** has had solo exhibitions in London, New York and Berlin. His next opens at Marlborough Fine Art London in March. **Terry Jones** teaches at Carlisle College. **Judith Kazantzis** received a Cholmondely Award in 2006. **John Kinsella** lives in Australia. **Chris Kinsey**'s second collection is *Cure for a Crooked Smile* (Ragged Raven, 2009). **Stephen Knight**'s book for children, *Sardines and Other Poems*, was published in 2004. **Lotte Kramer** has thirteen books, German and Japanese editions. **Glyn Maxwell** was short-listed for the 2009 Forward prize. TV journalist **Alex McRae** has an Eric Gregory Award. **James Midgley** also has an Eric Gregory. **Kim Moore** has had work accepted for publication recently in the *TLS*. **David Morley**'s next collection is *Enchantment* (Carcanet, autumn). **Roger Moulson**'s *Waiting for the Night-Rowers* won the Aldeburgh Prize. **Sheenagh Pugh** teaches at the University of Glamorgan. **Neil Rollinson**'s latest collection is *Demolition*. **John Siddique**'s fourth collection is *Recital – An Almanac* (Salt, 2009). **Anne Stevenson**'s latest collection is *Stone Milk* (2008). **Alan J Stubbs** was commended in the Arvon and shortlisted in the Bridport prizes. **Toon Tellegen**'s *Raptors* is forthcoming (Carcanet, Feb 2011). **Adam Thorpe** has published eleven works of fiction and five poetry collections. **Anthony Thwaite**'s edition of *Larkin's Letters to Monica* is due from Faber in September. **Chris Wallace Crabbe**'s latest collection is *Telling a Hawk from a Handsaw* (Carcanet). **Daniel Weissbort** was founder-editor of *MPT*. **Ben Wilkinson**'s pamphlet is *The Sparks* (tall-lighthouse, 2008). **Judith Wilkinson**'s translations of Tellegen are published by Shoestring. **Gregory Warren Wilson**'s fourth collection was *The Mercury Fountain* (Enitharmon, 2008). **Sarah Wardle** won the Geoffrey Dearmer Prize in 1999. *A Knowable World* appeared in 2009. **Susan Wicks**'s most recent collection is *De-iced* (Bloodaxe, 2007). **Sam Willetts**'s first collection is forthcomng from Cape. **Tamar Yoseloff**'s *Decorum* is forthcoming in 2011.

Geoffrey Dearmer Prize-winner Maitreyabandhu *lives and works at the London Buddhist Centre. He has been ordained into the Western Buddhist Order for nineteen years. In 2009 he won the Keats-Shelley Prize and the Basil Bunting Poetry Award. He has published two books on Buddhism.*

POEMS

It was a day like any other
when they came for us.
– Neil Rollinson

Chris Wallace-Crabbe
Up At A Villa

So, it felt alright at first, but now you rabbit on
expressing indisputable views on everything, in vivid
agreement with yourself, reinforcing the big Yes,
it having been determined that all popes and poets
can be no more than cocksuckers, arseholes, or merely both.
You smile with anger, red behind rimless glasses,
and right. Well, you could hardly be wrong, eh?
Even the pleasant CD cannot stem your fucking flow;
I wouldn't dare to try, I tell you that.
Why is all this display of petty power so important
now to you: pretty well always has been? And why
does the furious cortex hunger after correctness,
in just about everything? Buggered if I know,
but it must have been much like this
ever since you swaggered out of your wicker cradle
and set about ruling the world; you had the measure
of left and right, art, money, sexual deviation
and all the main current of thought –
yes, I'll have another splash of the red, why not.

Your garden flourishes outside in fruitful technicolour,
skillfully maintained, of course, by those expert hands
while you see through the cloudy glass of each political party
as well as the seamiest anti-semites and mining thugs,
because you smell the due stink in everything,
the dirt that rots every pocket. Yes, you are bloody well like
those puritans you affect to hate so much, thin churchy rats.
Every phony, you force us to understand, has been fattened up
on taxpayers' money. No scholar is not a fake,
bar those few honest sods you happen to endorse
or at least agree with, today: those commonly known
as your disciples, docile ephebes and victims,

who wouldn't answer back in a month of Sundays.
We admire your dense green gardening, drink on,
nary a soul half-daring to answer back or argue – after all
who wants his or her noggin blasted off with a phrase
like fart-warmed thunder? Certainly not yours truly.
We'll go on laughing then into the deep lull of evening.
After all, tomorrow we're driving back to the city.

That Which Is

Is? You could well say so.
Look, it all is.
Marvellous that it's like that for us.
                    Admit it, then:
We are surrounded by prodigious being,
By the isness that may be everything
Here and there,
Such universes of proffered being
Into which we are all of course destined
And it's no bad thing,
Given our wayward, wafting minds,
To have been granted extensive something
To take a firm grip on.
This anchors us.
This can embed us
In solid, colourful signs and music.
Flowers are good for us all.
Minerals do us no end of good,
All benevolent as the enormous twinklechart of stars.
These are the hither edge of being
And will survive our rotting in tombs,
Our return to the Is.

Glyn Maxwell
Calendar

Life in the care of memory is story.
Right around Christmastime it's Christmas story.
But I wake on a white sheet: January. If Christmas
comes now then I get it it's a miracle.

But February does, to the still alive, a sour
official at your side, he is on your side,
he never believed it really. He is dying
to confide in you he never believed it really.

Alfie turns twelve in March and that's all she wrote.
To say she's like this or is this, like you do in poems,
strikes me as time I could be in Sussex with her,
trampolining. Most things strike me as that.

On God I abstain like a poet. I do do Easter.
You are all, to the back teeth, paralysed in traffic
outside Emmaus, soon to be disabused
of the reasonable assumption that I'm dead now.

April's the blonde in a determined girl-band,
a daisy-chain of iPods: they went solo.
May was as undecided as it sounded.
June I would have in a heartbeat, pausing only

to think about it. Where the hell did *she* go?
Where the hell did they *all* go? Where did *I* go?
I am looking for something I had for a week in July
not last July this is but during the Cold War.

August went *hey man* so I went hey man,
anything going down later? And we just smoked
and trod our shadows. One of us said *those chicks
were really hot* I've a horrible feeling I did.

September is trying to empathise with pain
it causes. Everyone's old and everyone's new.
Someone in English says there's a star in the east!
Next morning you ask in Maths and he says it's a plane.

What you are going to have to endure one day
will look like a skull or a witch or a web or a ghost.
It will look like Halloween doesn't half start early
but it's actually last year's one metastasizing

gaily. Cue November the Seventh, all
I mean by miracle. That I up and made it.
My other great date I can honestly say I've not met.
I'm not talking (and sort of am) about Guardian Soulmates.

The years are clattering in from the icy fields
with what they've got. The first three next to nothing;
the next three three dumb furry things that are all
they loved; the next three? gifts you're kind of stuck with,

and all of the rest bring everything that's left
and hoist it high towards the glow. December's
welcome to this scene, the souls in circles
widening out into darkness warming each other,

thinking the glow does that when the glow does jack
but show you where to stare. And when I one day
find myself in a crush like that I'll hate it,
I'll elbow out to the edge where the light is gone

like the sun for Pluto, like that morning Pluto
learned it was not a planet so I took Pluto
out for some ales with everyone I've forgotten
in a dive so deep in the earth we were all Aussies.

Maitreyabandhu
Homecoming

If I had to think of a place
            I'd think of those cold shallows
                        where the dogs drank
and I threw a stick
and everything was patterned with sycamore. I'd think

            of myself as a child
                        falling asleep
in the back of the Austin Princess.

            I'd think of our being together
                        as a small thing –
picking up a windfall
or pouring a tumbler-full of water –
                        the moment, extended,
when an engine stops and time folds away.

            You were blurred,
                        as though through chlorine –
your rose-body wavered,
            breaking-up,
                        your limbs made ripples
when I spoke –

I was finding my feet in a place of undistraction.

            We were there together.
                        And it might have been
at the top of the garden
by the birch trees
            near the hole-in-the-hedge,
                        or it might have been anywhere
between traffic noise,
in the Sunday silence of the high street.

Roger Moulson
The Sea At Balbec

Have I time to revisit all those summers, those long periods,
for I need to rest as they lengthen over paragraphs and pages
before I turn to that parade of beauty on the promenade
or stand in the hotel dazzled by mirrors and refraction,
its light reflecting back the way I've come, and find myself
reading and rereading, missing the reassurance of line endings
in a cityscape of prose where I get lost again in passions
and soirees, a little breathless as the past moves to the present,
the present to the past, whose recollections merge with mine
as I see friends become the selves they'd always promised.
Then, if I have time, I'll breathe, and breast the sea at Balbec.

John Kinsella
What I Saw Off Cheynes Beach

Seeing the black eyes of white pointers
some people want to poke them, to take these sea-
giants out with one small finger, 'defensive'
mastery greater than dragging

sperm whales in from the continental
shelf, those old Norwegian chasers
cutting through a whale slipstream,
the passages they know. So, at five
years old I stand on the warped

white sands of the beach, holidaying,
looking out into the bay at the flagged
carcasses of whales, mountains in the blue-black
ocean, disturbed like a split lip spitting
froth and fear, bobbing though so lifeless

I wonder what living is, sand too cold
beneath my feet, too cold in my long pants
and windcheater, the stench of flensing
and boiling down, teeth piled high,
seawater and blood and spermaceti

of the whaling station — reason for the town —
reason for posturing against the French,
an American connection from the beginning
they wished to make, filling the oil-lamps
of readers in cities around the globe.

Seeing the black eyes of white pointers
I wonder if they are one-eyed, orbicular
to the one side, to keep an eye out,
thrusting up on to the dead whales, side-
swiping jaws ripping skin and blubber

and I know then blood comes out of the dead
though it flows differently – I've already
cut myself severely – and the dark ocean
makes a different viscosity, an attracting
and diluting flow that is scent for sharks

to follow in, to rasp atmosphere over great gills
as they emerge like dolphins, but ample and rough
and with a new take on grace: who is to say,
this beautiful flesh-death, death in death,
so energised as they bite the air, our seeing.

All of me, all of Mum, and all of Dad
would fit into one of those white pointers,
giant finned barrels propelling teeth,
but I don't think that at the time,
on the shore, looking out at the blue-black-red

collars of blood, the growing number
of sharks, the glut and the feast and the strange
angles of biting and tearing and looking at me
not so far away but far away from shark mind
so single-mindedly completing its plan,

its awareness, its line of thought: the news
I will tell the following year when I start school,
my grandfather in the spotter plane, the thrill,
the chase, the history of harpoons and the anger
it will make in me and the blood it will fill

me with that's not red but froths with history
and witness and a dull science that quells fear
and vengeance even though my brother
will surf where surfers are taken, are snatched,
all of them saying, 'leave them be,

these great creatures', the driven and logical
giants who know their own company
and the cartilaginous nature of ocean
so solid and flexible and churned up
with all that we call matter, all

that post-Enlightenment posturing
we laugh at and over in our secular
worship, those large blips on the sonar,
those seeing black eyes of white pointers.

Neil Rollinson
from Talking Dead

Time before and time after
                    – T.S. Eliot

The Wall

It was a day like any other
when they came for us.
This was the world we knew,
except the light was different:
the sky, the leaves, the distant sea.
We held hands as we walked,
and they walked behind us,
smoking cigarettes, talking
in hushed tones, embarrassed.
Only the colours troubled me,
the dandelions, how bright they were.
I hadn't noticed that before.
The world will carry on, you said,
but I wasn't sure. I had an intuition
that once I was gone
it was the end for everyone.
You gripped my hand as we came
to the wall. You were the one
true constant in everything.
The stone was warm, we could feel
the heat against our backs.
There was a scent of marjoram.
The sea was blue, and a single ferry
sailed out of the harbour.

Head-shot

It didn't hurt a bit, in fact
I felt ecstatic. I could see the bullet,
bright as a star. I could trace
its parabola over the field,
like fishing wire, a pencil line
drawn on paper.

I was, for a moment, a visionary.
I stilled the mayhem, the wind, the rain.
The bullet flew right through my head.
I went down like a sack of spuds,
sat on my arse in the shit.

I saw each of my friends
come and look at me.
Some were frightened
and some were full of life.
One held my face and kissed me.

I was far away, I thought of no one.
I was the only living thing in the universe,
and giddy with it all, godlike.
I'd do it again, and again. Yes.
Shoot me again. Oh shoot me again.

The Good Old Days

In the dark ages they took their time.
They knew about pain
and butchered you slowly, whistling
as they went. It was God's work.

The first few minutes were awesome.
I didn't know I could scream like that,
but nothing lasts forever,
soon the adrenalin kicks in and you're high

as a kite. The flesh comes off
like bark from a tree, the soul rises,
and the body breathes.

The Romans were worst: they'd let you live,
but slaughter your wife and child.
You can only suffer while the breath
runs through you, any torturer knows that.

The Bed

I opened my mouth to breathe,
like I do in dreams,
and the water flowed into me.
I sank like a stone.
At first I thought it was pain
but it was just
the beginning of bliss.
I could feel the buds in my throat
palpitate: the atavistic gills.
I saw the sand eel and tuna,
the plankton lifting in veils.
I breathed so deep I could taste
the salt and seaweed.
And I saw as I fell, the dark
hull of the ship above me,
its cold shadow. Things glittered
in the gloom like stars in the sky.
I saw dolphins, blue and green.
I was laid in the sand and the fish
came in thousands to pick me clean.
I loved the nights there,
the ultramarine, the moonlight,
the ghostly glow of the jelly fish
shifting like cloud above me.

Jane Hirshfield
Red Wine Is Fined By Adding Broken Eggshells

Red wine is fined by adding broken
eggshells or bull's blood,
but does not taste of the animal travelled through it.

Cold leather of fog on the day, then only the day,
cleared and simple,
whose windows lift equally into what light happens.

The dog asks to go out and you let her,
age rough in her coat as stairs that keep no landing.

The familiar is not safety.

Yet a horse unblindered runs back to the shape it knows burning.

The Dark Hour

The dark hour comes
in the night and purrs by my ear.
Outside, in rain,
the plush of the mosses stands higher.
Hour without end, without measure.
It opens the window and calls its own name in.

Sam Willetts
Starlings

Amazement as we walked together
in the cold of the year – a vast
reach of birds, nearing and ebbing past

understanding, numberless over the fields'
spires of shadow; now like iron filings
magnet-swept in three dimensions,

massing to a dark fold and spreading
light again; now a tidal gesture,
the opening and closing of a hand.

John Stammers
Like A Heatwave Burning

It was the hottest summer on record;
we flew into rages at the drop of a pin.
The heat made cacti of us all.

I woke up hot crazy at one in the morning.
The day's sun had heated up the sky so heavy
it felt like being ironed.

We sat on the curbside like hot bananas
and Jane read me the Miranda
of our future lives together:

there would be no future lives together.
I'd never heard the nightjay squawk
so damnably shrilly in the still, still stilly.

My eyeballs made sinuous rills.
I sloughed on my sandals and loped
onto a streetcar named expire.

Tyres welded cars to the road.
I got out my character
and began the tasks of a lifetime.

Pine trees collapsed in a dead swoon
all over the place. Believe you me,
honeydew features, it was hot.

Susan Wicks
Sorry

for Elkie

The sky itself is simple,
its winter end of afternoon
bleeding imperceptibly from slate to green.
Only the branches of the tree
cut it into thousands of lit pieces
shivering with the force of the wind.

This morning while your mother still breathed
you sat at her bedside, saying
Sorry, sorry, sorry, whether or not she could hear,
your words air
from a world that was already far away
and complicated, forking and forking with each new branch.
Now her body is already
simplifying itself.
Everything you both said, everything you were together
is thrashing, many-fingered, rain-drenched
as trees on the horizon.

Note: Phineas P. Gage (1823-1860) was a railroad construction foreman now remembered ↗
for his incredible survival of an accident which drove a large iron rod through his head,
destroying one or both of his brain's frontal lobes, and for that injury's reported effects
on his personality and social functioning – effects said to be so profound that friends saw
him as "no longer Gage".

James Midgley
Phineas survives

but all the clouds are anvils on his back.
On my back – is it my back? – I lean away
from my hands as if they are lizards.
Always those brown little lizards
would sun themselves in the parched air
by the tracks. Phineas summons rain
now, and here it pours. Its metal rounds
are one and a quarter inches in diameter.
Phineas drops to his knees and I reach
to pull him from the dirt,
but the lizards are under the hot sun and here
is the hot sun. We are a centre.
A bridge leans down to drink its river –
am I bait, then, ready for the hook?
Thunder overhead, underhead, in the head.
Phin, you've dropped your hammer.
I move to scoop it from the ground
but it figures my nails wrong and thuds.
Nothing hurts. Sneezing
hurts, sometimes. I will find myself
scattered in the grass near a pair of boots,
sat on a sleeper, inside the fireplace
that keeps the engine hurtling.
Small thoughts, you can come
out of hiding now. Goddamn it, Phin, goddamn.
And that too: Phineas has been god,
genius of a leaking faucet. To be expected.
In one of my memories I am looking at a skull
in a museum. In another I am a black eel
made of metal, ready to be thrown.
Phin, I say, Phin, come out of the tunnel, but
I cannot: speak or come out of the tunnel.
Some archer has drawn back my spine – release.

James Harpur
The Angels And The Harvesters

As thoughts arrive
from god knows where,
or winter sunlight
drops from clouds
and lights a patch
of trees, or grass,
they just appeared
from nowhere
among the harvesters
the field a world
of cutting, gathering
and desultory songs;
the edges of their forms
etched bright
they walked between
the bending figures
curious
pausing to watch
like ancestors
almost remembering
the world they'd left
or foreigners
amused to see
old ways persisting;
they moved around
invisible –
unless one glimpsed,
perhaps, light thicken,
a glassy movement,
as air can wobble
on summer days –

and then they went
walked into nothing
just left the world
without ceremony
unless it was
the swish of scythes
the swish of scythes.

Lynn Foote
January

The heron is tilted toward heaven; its nest
is like an upturned beehive. It must be warm
to drop down to the deep of it. A plane flies
through the blue band and is making its entirely
peaceful way across the sky – a blur of red, a flash
or logo. Another bird, its mate perhaps, soars past.

I wake up to the fact that all the birds are flying
in and out of each other, a tapestry of adoring flight
as swans muddle by. They know, as I don't, that
the seasons are on their way, there's no stopping them.
However many lives I had, it wouldn't be enough.

John Greening
Agny

To Edward Thomas

Edward, we're going to look for your grave
at Agny (something to do with sacrifice?).
I doubt somehow that we will find it
so off the beaten track.

                              But that was you,
to take the road less travelled. We wouldn't
expect you to be with the hordes of the dead
at Tyne Cot or on a wall of names.

You died at an observation post.
You looked and looked, and saw the detail
we do not.

                Today, there is a thick mist.
We head towards Beaurains to find you.

                    *

And here, beyond allotments, next to back
gardens where a Frenchman mows his lawn,
you are. And there the tall foliage
lours, and, yes, the speculative rooks
are chorusing you. Even – just then –
a woodpecker digging out its round hole
to hide in. P.E.THOMAS   POET

David Morley
Spinning

But these two things shall come to thee
in a moment in one day, the loss of children,
and widowhood: they shall come upon thee
in their perfection for the multitude of thy sorceries
and for the great abundance of thine enchantments.
 – Isaiah 47

1.

I love those stories when the world they wake
whitens on the horizon of your own eye
as though another sun has neared us in the night
or some new star flowered from the dark matter.
They shift on a single movement of mind or image –
a suicide leaps into space but lands on a high ledge
where he is found by fishermen with ropes and jokes.
The man says he thought the night was his own death
and it was, nearly. His hair has sprung into white fright
as if his head had been dipped into the dyes of the dawn.

What's expected of me, more so because unexpected,
is that I will go on telling and making and spinning,
more so because I was guilty of the crime called happiness.
Stories for children when we know all of us are children.
And now I possess only my own poised possession
that I shall deliver these tales from some darker attention.
There they squat around the fires, with their teeth glittering.
They are moving on from their roll-ups to their shared pipes,
from red wine to glugs of gold whiskey. They are settling in
as if they were waiting for some long haul between settlements.

They say language shows you, so my stories should show you
what worlds I've wound through, whose voices I've breathed in –
that smoke spooling from their mouths; the fire's smoke
swirling above them make an understood utterance, a ghost
of what we see, what we pass through and what might be watching
us watching ourselves waiting. If that's too curdled for you
try truth. A five year-old boy dies. His parents bide by his body
for three days. Then they fill a rucksack with his best-loved toys.
Another rucksack embraces the child's body. They drive to a cliff,
hitch on the rucksacks and throw themselves spinning off the earth.

What does their tale say about how much they loved each other
and how much their son loved and was loved? Their story
makes something cease in you. They drove as if going on holiday
in a campervan. They say language shows you, and this story
shows to me that truth and even love grow impossibly possible.
This is not what you have come for. It is not what you wanted.
Where is the magic-eyed metaphor that reverses them into life?
Why am I not spilling word-lotions into your ears that allow
these three loving people to meet in another place, laughing
and singing and unbroken? Why doesn't the story wake the boy?

My own story interests nobody, not now I'm on my own.
Making story costs them nothing but my drink and caravan.
It's the hour before I begin when the clouds close down
and I'm lacking of language and in a desert of image
and nothing knows nothing. I am not even nowhere.
Now the word-trail slows in my mind, my blood sheds
all sugar and I can recognise no thing, not even the walls
of my van, or who I am, or what I will later, maybe, become.
I used to reach out at these times, touch my wife and say
'my wife'; then I would come back. I would come back into life.

2.

The fire may as well be language for translating the logs
from their green, spitting blocks into red pictures and paintings.
The children spy wide worlds from the ringside of the fireside
as if a circus were performing before them. It shows in their eyes
for it is all reflected there. I usually start the evening with a call
to calm, then a joke and a drink before I unleash the animals.
Animal tales first, padding around the fire just there in the dark,
now in the ring of light, and back again; I go out of sight
for the ending. Then stories about witches (the children dozing)
and so on to burkers and ghosts before night swallows my voice.

They say language shows you but subject shows you too.
Reverse that order of telling and you end up killing the evening,
sending the children unarmed into nightmare, startling
the rabbits of the audience with glare of monster and murder.
Yet one day, one day I shall never be there, not that I am now.
I stalk that ring of light. I know to toe around every twig.
I know when to lower my voice, and when to stop silent.
That's when I let natural magic have its effect – an owl call;
a dog fox wooing demonically in the wood; badgers scratching
and sputtering. These are not words; they are warier than words.

They are life not legend and sometimes they flout me.
They do not enter on cue. They make witty what is deadly
or horror from humour. Control. Do I really want control?
When their hearts are hearing me while their eyes are on the fire
it is as if I were the fire's brother, that we were a double act.
The fire came free (although children fed it until sleep).
Just pictures and paintings. We'd see them anyway in dreams.
What's expected of me is that I feed their dreams, lobbing
green blocks of words that spit and split and charm and char
while all the long, wordy night I am desperate to be doused.

What's fabulous might be a hedgehog spiny with rhyme
or a bride born from gnarled nouns. What's fabulous might be
darkness drowsing over a woman of words beside a waterfall
of words. What's fabulous might be an anvil hammered white-hot
with hurt, or Lipizzans held or hurtling on the harness of a verb.
Truth or tale, you've winnowed my mind many times too many
for me to be free with feigning, and now night's met my heart
and halved it. This is something I cannot say tonight, for tonight
is my last night. Tonight at midnight I am laying down my words.
I shall bury them beneath the embers of that brother, the fire.

I am sloughing the freight of fiction, the shackling story.
l owe this to my wife for believing in the one truth of me.
I am leaving the camp by dawn. I am taking nothing
apart from myself. The enchantment I offered as payment,
they will find it under fire. They will shovel it out ashen,
riven beyond repair. Stories are second chance. They repair.
They repay. I am broken. I want to try the truth.   So,
I am glad you are all here. I hope you enjoy your evening.
I was here all the time listening to you but now it's my turn.
Ladies and gentleman, and children. I am ready when you are ready.

Anthony Thwaite
Ancestors

My father traced our ancestors for years
Through parish registers and censuses and wills,
Took photographs of gravestones, learned to read
Crabbed secretary hand, transcribe each thing
From inventories, distinguishing in red
The illegitimate from children born
In wedlock, puzzling out the muddled names
Vergers misheard as year succeeded year
And the meshed generations spun like spiderwebs.

My father died thirty-one years ago.
Up in the attic, stacked in musty boxes, sit
His precious notebooks, genealogies,
Family trees, even a coat-of-arms
He asked a Herald to construct to show
That we were once armigerous – how vain
In every sense... Now, in my eightieth year,
The whole accumulation weighs me down.
I have no time now for my ancestors.

Toon Tellegen
My father fished for answers...

My father
fished for answers, found none,
but he sang

real fishermen float in silence, crowned with glory,
with their bellies up, like chairmen of boards
drifting out to sea

my father sang about patient endurance
and about hunger that gnawed at him,
wanted something of him,
refused to tell him what it was

grinding his teeth while he sang softly

and my mother heard him
and took him with her –
didn't tell him where –
pushed him gently backwards on a bed,
nestled herself on top of him

and they became entangled
in the space that stretched beyond the furthest stars
                        and induced the deepest sleep,
the great slovenly unknown.

Translated by Judith Wilkinson

David Grubb
Kansas

The good people of Kansas come out of sleep
and wander into the banquet called breakfast
and the day calls and sun begins and birds.

The good people of Kansas do this because
there is no other way and God has made grass
and America is a kite that flies above the world.

The good people of Kansas are not afraid of work
and if somebody comes to the door it may well be
the boy Jesus who has a problem with a miracle;

and they will take him in and help him fix it and then
watch the story on television and read about it in the
evening news and never ever stop telling their friends;

until the next time somebody comes to their door with
a broken angel or a dead dog or a story about how their
baby has become a booby and surely $1,000 will fix it;

the sky becoming low and the rain always and didn't
they go to the same church years ago and what a mess
religion has become and even the trees acting strange.

The new billboard says IF YOU CAN – KANSAS CAN
and farmers still ride into the horizon but we never see
them return, their faces like old paper bags, full of empty.

Rainer Maria Rilke
Apparition

What is pushing you back today
into the restlessly waving garden
through which a shower of sunlight
has just been walking? Look,
how behind him the green grows more serious.
Come! Like you I would like to ignore
the weight of trees.
(If one of them broke across the path
one would have to call for men
to lift it up. What is
so heavy in this world?)
You came cleanly down the many
stone steps: I heard you.
Here again you are without sound.
I am alone with my hearing,
with the wind... suddenly
a nightingale climbs up
in the sheltered shrub.
Listen, in the air, how it stands,
crumbling or not ready. You,
do you hear it with me, you –
or are you concerned now
with the other side of the voice
turning away from us?

Translated by Lotte Kramer

Sarah Wardle
Keeping Going

Dawn spills relief after a long night. On a sill
hyacinths greet white sky. Now Big Ben
is striking seven o'clock and the streetlamps

die together with stairwell lights in the council
highrise and a bulb above the No Entry sign.
I feel like a Fresher returning from the river,

where I caught a crab while I watched
the swans, my Latin prose still not yet done
for a tutorial at half-past nine. And you

don't need anti-depressants. Morning
sun is enough, the pace of eight o'clock
pavements, the urgency of Victoria station,

fifteen minutes at a coffee stand, a blue
sky high enough to dream into, the sharp
air of a January platform, frosted fields

seen from a train, a walk uphill, a face
you know, even just as an acquaintance,
a shared joke, shoots at an office window.

Sheenagh Pugh
Trondheim: January

You try to get a handle on this town
and it comes back to the hooded crows

foraging in snow, as everyday as sparrows,
but civil: no brawls. Grey-robed, black-capped, they wait

by the Justice Museum where the hangman's receipt
lists prices; so many kroner to take off

a hand, a head. They venture a throaty laugh
at the children sledging downhill

from the fort, do sentry-go outside its wall,
where the resistance men lay in their blood.

By the frozen river they promenade,
their suits shabby-genteel against the white:

elderly flaneurs in the strange pink daylight,
trading reminiscences, now and then.

Stephen Knight
Thank You For Having Me

everyone's packing up everyone's going home
the girl guides and the traffic wardens all the souls
the neighbourhood has harboured downing placards
turning signs like *PUKKA-PIES... they're delicious* CLOSED
CLOSED EVERYTHING MUST GO the dummies stripped of clothes
don't mourn them uselessly [something something something]
men whose shoulders sink a little further from their ears
hail cabs or wait for buses Dora *¡vāmonos!*
The Ink Spots old poor Johnnie Ray The Prince of Wails
The Nabob of Sob running like a younger man
the boy in fluffy slippers and the men on stilts
lolloping past the locksmiths outside New Cross station
HARRY & SON established 1960 now
where are you Harry everyone's going home
it's raining in this poem here come on let's shelter
underneath these rough-and-tumble alexandrines
yonder raindrops dripping off an overhanging word
shaken from umbrellas under awnings *allons-y*
the pink girl in the boob tube in the first class carriage
insects from the cracks in paving stones conquistadores
in tarnished [technical term for piece of armour]
bankers vendors Captain Cook home before it's dark
before the lights are necessary in houses where the chairs
hold out their puffy/threadbare arms to take them in
everyone's leaving clickdripclickdropclickdripclickdrop
so many footsteps now or shadows rounding corners
bone-dry box-shaped holes in car parks everywhere
we have to go home in the end leave the swings
to hang their heads strap you in then steer you back
through the spring tide's twigs and plastic see the river
cross that road we took not long ago

Chris Kinsey
from Appointments With Hades

Sing A Song Of Sixpence

Mashed potato moons. Beetroot. Spam.
Class time and playtime blur –

slurring rules: *i. before e. except after c.,*
'You change the sign of the bottom line and add.'

I wanted a *'green hill far away'*
much more than to *'Fight the good fight',*

or to take turns skipping rhymes:
My boyfriend's name is Fatty

He lives in Sialatti.
369 the goose drank wine...

Crazes I didn't share: Batman. French Crochet.
Pomegranates: *Don't step on the cracks. One for sorrow...*

Progress Papers for *11 plus. A First Aid in English*:
A gaggle of geese. A pride of lions.

Cassius Clay. Muhammad Ali: *Float*
like a butterfly, sting like a bee.

Words from the *Telly* stalked our vocabulary:
Moors Murderers, Assault, Abduction.

Instructions hissed without sing-song:
Don't take sweets from strangers.

Don't get into cars.

Kim Moore
The Wolf

She wants you to lie down with the wolf,
the one who eats chalk to make his words
as white as snow, so each letter lands
in a puff of smoke, the one who likes red,
who stays in bed so long he could become
just another pattern in the wallpaper.

She wants you to lie down with the wolf,
the one she has clothed in wool
from the mountain sheep, the one who is not
as he appears, the one who treads time
beneath his paws which are always
caked in flour, the one the children sing of.

If you lie down with the wolf, the one who carries
the wind in his belly, the one who can take
a house from you, the one who hides in shadow
so the boy who cries wolf is a liar, she'll stroke
your hair and smile secrets at you, slit him open
and fill him with stones and watch you both sink.

Leah Fritz
Whatever Sends The Music Into Time

Whatever sends the music into time,
not just in metre but through centuries,
Mozart years of sound, the flat stone skipped
across the glassy surface of that fourth
transparency; whatever it may be,
code as tight as DNA or heavenly gift,

perhaps a curse, but if a curse a gift
for some poor devil in the mind of time –
what I am getting at, it cannot be
within one's sole control – the centuries
roll back, old ground uncovered, a fourth
of history returns, the rest is skipped

to be revealed again when more is skipped
under the stone where earth's most treasured gift
lies buried waiting the tiller's bringing forth
each truth in its appointed (random) time.
And so the influence of centuries
gone by foreshadows what is yet to be.

But here I am concerned with what *will* be
when my pen, across the pages skipped,
auditions for its place in centuries.
How does a poet hint for such a gift
and to whom? Mother of future time,
where do I seek you? In Einstein's fourth

dimension? Or in myself, which can give forth
such music as I have? Let it be
enough for me and mine in our own time.
About that time – about the days I skipped
through city leaves, thinking the sun a gift
immeasurable, no thought of centuries,

no knowledge then of years (of centuries
and histories, less intimation): if forth
from infancy comes all there is of gift,
struggle though I may; if it should be
my name in that long heritage is skipped
for one less happy in her own true time,

I think the music that I hear must be
enough, the other vanity well skipped.
Sufficient beauty is there in my time.

A.J. Stubbs
Oedipus

sun was a straight white line coming
in at the cracked lip of the front door
silently, even the birds were standing
wait on dog slates toeing an edge of gutters
and rooftops, and looking out from here
for what might break fast of night, or
shake free and warm a cold blood
uncertainly brooding in the air, would
sip out things before leaving the lair
to clothe itself in soiled leaves, and pass
black hole eyes that draw down energies
lashing out and making violent seas,
perforating all of those honeycomb
doors locked up and named a home

Judith Kazantzis
Mrs Blake's Poem

for Enitharmon Press's Fortieth Birthday

There now, elements of pain and rage,
and beauty: got stuck in his throat

Long long ago
the lion lay down with me
under the palm-tree in the garden

His sturdy meaty lamb,
I pulled the beauty
like stringy old beans out of his sore throat
line by line
There now, like – a red flannel!

He laughed at me
flung the flannel dramatically
into the lavender
I discreetly skipped out of the way
as it were, into the shady fold
of the page

How we loved our garden.

Arthur Boyars
In Memoriam David Drew

The sea is only borrowed,
Like the sky, like memory itself,
Like friends and children;
These will not last

As real presences. They start
Fading, before we have
Them fixed in occupying space,
Before we start the count

And wonder what time is given us
For company, in this grim, lonely place,
What time for sun and daylight
Before long darkness falls,

And we are hustled back to our origin,
To that unthinking place
Where all is quite forgotten
As if it all had never been!

Adam Thorpe
JÄÄÄÄR

That it means 'the edge of ice'
in Estonian is hardly a surprise:
the melting away of consonants,
the freezing of vowels into a howl. Once

the entire bay would be tundra from November;
now it's slush, and snow something to remember...
I see the 'r' approaching the 'y' sound
of the start, with less and less of that ice-bound

middle part I am incapable of pronouncing right
(the skater toppling, the fledgling's first flight
too soon after winter): the Baltic lapping higher
until all that's left is a tiny, fish-hook cry.

BEES

Terry Jones
Bee

i
It's a matter of where you tread
nothing is hurt nothing touched
if you missed the nest
hid under the iron hearts of flowers
scaffold eyes on a root
and until you heard it
your ear would be in the dark
a bee coming in on unsettlable drone
for its version of the sweet

ii
one I locked in a bottle
settle and lifted its furious resonance
held on the draught of itself
where it hung then hit and hit
the inconceivable
atheist on an invisible wing
without dying a bee
will save its sting
for the real

iii
is it saying 'am' or 'om'
after its dance zooming
east or west?
hand curled in yellow-black fur
you could ride a bee
to the holy doorway of its hive
hold the note and enter

David Briggs
In The Senior Common Room

A swarm without a hive has no master.
— Law of the Roman Republic

The Divinity master kept bees: his apiary set
beyond the Second Eleven's outfield,
at the gorse-hedged limit of the grounds.
Long, summer afternoons they watched him
going among hives through wedged-shadows,
and those who couldn't hold a bat straight

opted 'off Games' to go to the honeybee
and learn how diligent she is.
The breaking of the comb-honey's wax capping
was what they came to cherish –
an Arcadian crème brûlée
they smeared on hot crumpets, spooned into tea

those autumn nights in the oak-panelled study.
He told them bees were blessed when leaving Eden,
became handmaids of the Most High;
how Bretons believed them the tears of Christ crucified;
how they sang 'Hosanna in Excelsis'
on the stroke of midnight each Christmas Eve,

for which he blessed them with slabs of fondant.
They wore the angry blotches on their knuckles
proudly; and, when a swarm of errant drones,
drunk on gorse-flowers, flew a careless scrawl
through the lunch-hall window,
to rummage among the treacle puddings,

and prompt HM – worn beyond patience
by years of bee-related complaint –
to pronounce, "Since you cannot control them,
these pests are no more welcome here
than disease," they replied, "But
how do you know they're *our* bees?"

Gregory Warren Wilson
At That Impressionable Age

every single image was a two-part invention;
I set about catching my own self-consciously
in an improvised trap – three angled mirrors
that deflected me me me to infinity and back.

Paul Henry
Ring

I can't get the ring out of my finger.
How long till it disappears
this ghost ring, twenty years deep?
I'm branded. Is it the same with you?
Your fingers were slenderer than mine.

NOW AND THEN

Ben Wilkinson
Now And Then

This poem I've just found, sorting through old junk,
still conjures something up, despite its hopeless flaws –

'*hot summer*'; '*dragonflies darting above flowers*';
'*the peacefulness of water*'; '*a balloon lifting off* –

as if a door swung half-open - '*blackbirds singing*';
'*white clouds drifting*' – then suddenly pulled shut.

      *

While somewhere out there, so many miles off,
I'd wager you're imagining anything but

those days spent on that borrowed canal boat.
But I wonder if I dropped this poem in the post

what you'd think – our dutiful cards at Christmas,
birthdays, the odd email, then something like *this*?

      *

No matter: though I reckon myself a better poet now,
I can't pick the lock. It gives up these glimpses –

'*glittering skyline*' – then closes like a book. Or like
the one thing, if little else, you'd surely remember –

those photos we took on the water that weekend,
before I
        stumbled and dropped in your camera...

Liz Berry
In The Steam Room

Here, any body
    might give you pleasure:
feet, shoulders, stomachs jewelled with veins
are sexless
   in the fug

which softens muscles to plasticine, slickens
freckled city skin,
    liquefies flesh
until shapes shift,
   and we are all vapour

scorch-breathed and boundary-less,
filling the room
    in white waves of perspiration,
our tongues nuzzling the neck
     of the fat man
on the bench, easing
    beneath the breasts
of the beautiful girl
    in the dripping blue swimsuit,

every pore an invitation,
    every mouth, ear,
nostril, arse hole, rich anemoned seabed of cunt
a place for joy,

cells loosening and yielding in the heat,
    slackening
into pleasure
   deeper
    then deeper
to that bodiless moment
    when atoms met
and life gasped
   I'm coming, I'm coming
in the darkness.

Alex McRae
In St Paul's Cathedral With My Father

Hard to imagine a communion here –
to kneel and wait with eyes cast down, not up,
under this perfect unsupported dome
while tourists swirl past. Tucked up in the gods,
you and I roost like owls in swooping space
that drops away beneath us when we lean
to look at those left earth-bound, far below.

We have kept this morning for each other.
You're on the far side of the gallery
cupping your mouth close to the curving wall,
and though your back is to me, I still hear
your whispered *Any luck?* – as if you were
beside me – and wave, to show I've understood.

Dorothy Sargent Rosenberg Annual Poetry Prizes, 2010

Prizes ranging from $1,000 up to as much as $25,000 will be awarded for the finest lyric poems celebrating the human spirit. The contest is open to all writers, published or unpublished, who will be under the age of 40 on November 6, 2010. Entries must be postmarked on or before the third Saturday in October (October 16, 2010). Only previously unpublished poems are eligible for prizes. Names of prize winners will be published on our website on February 5, 2011, together with a selection of the winning poems. Please visit our website www.DorothyPrizes.org for further information and to read poems by previous winners.

CHECKLIST OF CONTEST GUIDELINES
- Entries must be postmarked on or before October 16, 2010.
- Past winners may re-enter until their prizes total in excess of $25,000.
- All entrants must be under the age of 40 on November 6, 2010.
- Submissions must be original, previously unpublished, and in English: no translations, please.
- Each entrant may submit one to three separate poems.
- Only one of the poems may be more than thirty lines in length.
- Each poem must be printed on a separate sheet.
- Submit two copies of each entry with your name, address, phone number and email address clearly marked on each page of one copy only.
- Include an index card with your name, address, phone number and email address and the titles of each of your submitted poems.
- Include a $10 entry fee payable to the Dorothy Sargent Rosenberg Memorial Fund. (This fee is not required for entries mailed from outside the U.S.A.)
- Poems will not be returned. Include a stamped addressed envelope if you wish us to acknowledge receipt of your entry.

MAIL ENTRIES TO: Dorothy Sargent Rosenberg Poetry Prizes, PO Box 2306, Orinda, California 94563, USA

Tamar Yoseloff
Where You Are

The river bursts its banks,
spills over the map,
over names of farms and towns,
faded and cracked, the paper
eroding in your hands.

The stones you gathered
on the beach, the trinkets
stockpiled so you would remember
have lost their shine
torn from their source.

You had a mind of summer,
tarmac scalding your feet,
the red stain of the sun,
nothing left but a small pile
of ash, a fire

extinguished – a wound
in the ground. Everything
has floated away: trees, roads,
houses, a world of water,
colours seeped to white,

sharp light of forgetting;
the way he grows pale
behind your eyes,
loses definition, as you
let him go.

Tom Gilliver
from Apocalypso

I
it will be like living in the greenhouse again,
failing to comprehend the plants' simple needs
and re-learning the sound of feet on gravel –

baffled, perhaps, by the subtlety of sand
(for these adoptions, no root is too thin)
but thankful for acceptance into the family

(a surrogate mother and mute, scented children)
frail lily faces, white and forgetful as
if even the pastoral could be redeemed –

look!
a crowd of slender legs:
antelope on the golf course!
their serious faces shame the clean grass

Daniel Weissbort
Adam

I balance on a surface seems solid enough.
I know, however, that underneath it
agitates a self-regarding magnitude.
And I'm on board a gigantic back,
its movements disturbing depths within.
At any moment, it might draw me down.
Meanwhile, I observe sky which might be siphoned off,
flora over which shutters might close.
Each step, each breath taken in ignorance,
as if I were the Adam.

Anne Stevenson
Now

Every spring renews the blackbird for me
just when he claims the season for himself,
as out of the clear well of his voice I heft
with a longer rope a deeper memory.

After Words

Having lived long and softly
in the office of my head
     with its rules to scold me,
I didn't know I was unhappy
until you said... I said...
     when my tears told me.

ENCOUNTERS

[...] beauty does not exist in isolation; beauty only manifests itself in brief glimpses or enters into a relationship with the chaotic, the fragmented, the disharmonious etc., which of course are all part of everyday life.

– Pia Tafdrup

Four Mexican Poets

RESEARCHED AND INTRODUCED BY JOHN SIDDIQUE

TRANSLATED BY ROBERTO CANTU

A few years back, I heard the wonderful Mexican poet Coral Bracho speaking on a radio programme from the US. You know how it can be when a poetic voice really hits you? I was stunned by the richness of her language and the ecstasy in her lines. I immediately sought out her only book available in translation, which is a selected poems for the American market called *Firefly Under The Tongue* (New Directions). The book, and the sound of her reading voice, took me into one of those beautiful literary love affairs we sometimes have with authors. I poured over her words in English, reading the poems aloud, reading the Spanish as best I could, and imaginatively overlaying Coral's voice so that I could swim around in her sound, words and poetry. I started thinking that her work needed to be available to more people in the English-speaking world. For me its discovery was far more exciting than what I was reading in many of the magazines I subscribe to, or read at the Poetry Library. But not knowing how to begin to get her work seen, and not being a linguist or translator, I put the idea aside.

Later that year I was invited to read at a huge poetry festival in India, where I discovered that there were three Mexican poets on the programme: Rocío González, Araceli Mancilla Zayas, and Natalia Toledo. I made a beeline to their readings and made sure I met them over the course of the festival. I enjoyed all three poets, but Natalia Toledo touched something very profound in me, in a way that was similar to how Coral's work had. Her poetry was if anything more naked and sinuous. The English translations at the festival were useful for gaining access to the work, but had obviously been done in a hurry, and with a little too many of the various translators' fingerprints on their surfaces. I knew that a much better job could be done, and again this idea arose of trying to present some of this work to the English poetry audience. For selfish purposes, too, I simply want to read more of these poets. Amazingly, it turned out that Rocío knew Coral very well, and I begged for a contact address. I wrote a fan letter to her, putting forward the idea that I'd like to present her work and that of the three other poets in the UK. Of course I was going to struggle with the translation, but I thought that the universe would provide an answer if I committed to the project.

Things began to move to allow this to take place. I was asked to spend some time in Los Angeles by the British Council, and thought I might be able to find a co-pilot for my project there. Good fortune brought me to Professor Roberto Cantu, who is Distinguished Professor of Chicano Studies at California State University – where I was carrying out my residency. Roberto loves poetry and is exceptional in being capable of giving up his ego to serve the work at hand. He challenged me to do the same, and my role became one of producer, archivist and enabler for the work. We had a few heated meetings as we started working. All four poets had kindly sent me work, and Roberto and I got carried away by the texts and images. Roberto's ability to remain in the spirit of the poem is quite something. I added my take on poetic sensibility where I could, and both of us turned to the great Octavio Paz's work on poetics, *The Bow and The Lyre*, as a touchstone for the project.

It was Roberto who introduced me properly to Paz – and now my reading diet has a lot more openness to it. Working on these pieces, and sharing just a few of them here, has influenced my own writing immensely. I had already begun work on the follow-up to my latest book, *Recital*, whilst I was in LA, but Paz's ideas on poetics, together with Coral and Natalia's ability to approach the heart of meaning directly through deep metaphor, have caused me to go right back to opening considerations of what it means to be a poet. A good poem changes us forever when we encounter it; yet it is very easy to get fixed with an idea that we know what a poem is when we stick to just a few sources of poetry. Read lots of modern British poetry and you'll have a certain set of ideas about what a poem can be. But Paz argues that just because something is written as a sonnet, has the right rhymes, number of lines, syllabic count etc, doesn't mean that it is a poem. Outward forms do not make poetry: it's the heart of meaning, the text – and the poet's ability to use language to bring some aspect of human experience, the world and life, into a contained form – which lives and breathes inside the reader. And so I hope you find something new, or perhaps something very old, in this handful of pieces.

Coral Bracho
It Plumbs Its Own Depths And Stirs

A wave of dense light, intact fire.
A current, a soft breeze
that incites all, that scorches and unleashes,
that purifies everything
down to its intimate lines. In high tide the waterfall
casts the sun to its abyss (its constellated detachment, its joyous,
sustained
fall, its igneous
primal origin of crystals: digging furrows, opening trails,
fording,   sinking). The depths open
on the surface.
                    – The entire
ocean and calm
where it cradles, all that sand in its scorching density,
made fallow, turned to salt, plumbs its own depths
and stirs.

Rocío González

Marguerite Duras used to quote a passage by Jules Michelet where he recorded – relying, I suppose, on trustworthy sources – that during the Crusades or feudal battles, women would remain confined to their solitude for extended periods of time, overseeing their farms and, because of the absence of inter-subjective contact, that they began talking to themselves or to engage trees and animals in idle talk, and that perhaps they also sang or stretched the wind taut or festooned the arrows. And the spontaneous act began to turn into a habit, a custom which no one opposed, that no female neighbour questioned; on the contrary, many participated gladly in such practice; however, when men returned and found women talking with birds and foxes, they felt fear, the female discourse impressed them as insane, intolerable, and that's when witchcraft was born, or better yet: that's when the accusation was thrown against that incomprehensible language, born of women. This source teaches us that oftentimes the difference between discourses is a matter of life and death.

Araceli Mancilla Zayas
The Crossing

The sea is the rock's silence
      and blue is the form
      of the formless.
That entire sea halts at the light,
      the void moves it,
      stands vigilant.
That sea eternally enclosed.
      Everlasting fish swim en route to
      a yellow boundary
where delicate green on the verge,
      iridescent sun,
penetrate the depths.
      The roar of a sea with no waves
that rocks and sways,
      notwithstanding,
on a glance.
      It is a god within
or a mermaid on haunches.
      Its hues dissolve,
its arms
      are glimpsed
amid reefs.
Or it is only the light of an ocean
enraged in the distance.
      Beings of light
under a mind
that navigates

      the true waters.

Natalia Toledo
Ni guicaa T.S. Eliot

Ndaani' batanaya' gule jmá guie' naxiñá' rini
ziula' ne sicarú,
qui zanda gusiaanda' dxiibi guxhanécabe naa guirá ni gule niá'.
Guzaya' xadxí ne batanaya'
bitiide' guidilade' ra dxá' beñe
ne ndaani' guielua' bidxá yuxi nuí.
Gula'quicabe láya' Mudubina
purti' gule' luguiá nisa.
Guriá yaachi naxí gudó yaa' ti beenda' cayacaxiiñi' naa
ne guca' Tiresias biníte' guielua',
qui niquiiñe' guni'xhí' ora guzaya' stube ndaani' ca dxí ma gusi.
¿Guná nga ni bisanané binniguenda laanu?, ¿xí yuxi guie
bisaananécabe laanu?
Ca xiiñe' zutiipica' diidxa' guní' jñiaaca'ne zazarendaca'
sica ti mani' ripapa ndaani' guí'xhi', ne guiruti zanna tu laaca'.
Guirá beeu nuá' neza guete'
balaaga riza lú nisa cá tini, ni rini' xcaanda' guielua' pe'pe' yaase'.
Zabigueta' zigucaaxiee xquidxe',
ziguyaa xtube xa'na' ti baca'nda' ziña,
chupa bladu' guendaró ziaa' zitagua'.
Zadide' laaga' neza luguiaa, ni bi yooxho' qui zucueeza naa, zindaaya' ra
nuu jñiaa biida' ante guiruche guirá beleguí.
Zaca' xti bieque xa badudxaapa' huiini'
ni riba'quicabe guie' bacuá íque laga,
xa ba'du' ruuna niidxi sti guie'
zabigueta' xquidxe' ziaa' si gusianda' guie lúa'.

Note: This original is given in Zapotec, an indigenous Mexican language.

To T.S. Eliot

Red flowers blossomed on my hands
long and beautiful,
how can I forget the fear when I was dispossessed of all my certainties.
I walked on my hands
and wedged my body where there was mud
my eyes swelled with fine sand.
I was known as the girl with the water lilies
because my root was on the water's surface.
But I was also bitten by a snake that mated near the estuary
was blinded and became Tiresias who coursed history without a rod.
Which are the roots that germinate, which the branches that sprout from scrap?
Perhaps I am the last branch that will speak Zapotec
my children will have to whistle their language
and shall be homeless birds in the woods of oblivion.
I am in the South during all seasons
a corroded ship dreamt by my eyes black like the jicaco:
to my country I will return to smell its earth, I will dance under a deserted bower,
I shall be there to eat two things.
I will cross the plaza, the North will not detain me, I will embrace my Grandma
on time and before the last star descends.
Once again I will be the girl who displays a yellow petal on her right eyelid,
the girl who weeps milk of flowers
I will return to heal my eyes.

Jicaco: a fruit tree native to Mexico's Oaxaca region.

The Body Always Has At Least One Wound

PIA TAFDRUP INTERVIEWED BY RUTH O'CALLAGHAN

Pia Tafdrup (b. Copenhagen 1952) is a member of the Danish Academy and the European Academy of Poetry. Her awards include Nordic Council's Literature Prize in 1999 and, in 2006, the Nordic Prize from the Swedish Academy. Tafdrup has written thirteen collections of poetry; published here are: *Spring Tide* (Forest Books 1989), *Queen's Gate* (Bloodaxe 2001) and *Tarkovsky's Horses* (Bloodaxe 2010). She has also published *Walking over the Water* – a poetics – two plays and two novels. Her poems have been translated into more than thirty languages. *Thousandborn: The Poet Pia Tafdrup* is from Cosmo Films.

ROC: Unlike most other young children you were fascinated by the letters rather than the images – cow, pig etc – that are usually attached to them. Could you elaborate on this early learning experience?

PT: Long before I started school I was deeply moved by the sight of letters. The first I saw were of course my parents' handwriting. My father wrote almost in a Gothic style, very long letters, while my mother's letters were circular... How could they read each other? It was a mystery.

My parents met in England after the Second World War. Both of them had had to escape to Sweden from 1943 to 1945 because of their Jewish background: my mother with her family and my father with his mother, brother and sister. So the first thing they both dreamt of after the war was to travel freely and see the world. My mother often told me about how they met in London. The first time my father visited her she stayed in a pension close to Hotel Alexandra in Earls Court. She rented a room because she worked for a period in a bookshop called Bumpus in Oxford Street. When my father came to her she was writing Christmas cards. My father just sat there admiring her write these cards. So I guess hand-written letters have always had a special attractive force for me. That's why I usually start my poems with a hand-written draft.

When I was a child, my mother not only showed me the letters of the alphabet, she also made bookmarks where, with a needle, she pricked out letters I could sew. I sewed these designs, quite simple words like "light" (*lys*), "father" (*far*) etc: almost a magic process. Because I found written letters so fascinating, I invented a new alphabet as soon as I'd learned the alphabet in school. It was a secret code I shared with two classmates, until the day we were compromised and had to read our letters aloud.

I was fascinated by letters, but images also had a certain influence...

Were there other early influences that later had bearing on your work?
I clearly remember a situation when I was four years old and took part in the first philosophical discussion of my life. Because blood was streaming from my knee, which I had grazed, the theme was: *Why do we have to die?* My father was tying his tie in front of the mirror and I was sitting on the edge of a yellow bed-settee examining the phenomenon of blood. My father tried to comfort me with the words, "The body always has at least one wound". This is the first whole sentence I remember – but it didn't comfort me, it was a shock! In my ars poetica, *Walking Over Water*, I quote it as a statement central to my work. I'm not only thinking of the physical wound, but also of the fact that illusions burst. Even when we are really happy something hurts deep inside us. This early knowledge has been elaborated in many dimensions.

Your debut collection When An Angel Breaks Her Silence *(1981) takes the poetry beyond simple reflections by a young woman into metaphorical realms encompassing the relationship between body and soul.*
A central passage from Rilke says: *For the beautiful is nothing but the start of the terrible, which is what we can just bear.* Rilke's angel is not beautiful, it is terrible. It is the notion which today we call the sublime. The two opposing categories, the beautiful and the terrible, have been symptomatic of the idea of beauty since French Symbolism broke with the classical aesthetical ideals. Even today, my poems aim for beauty, well aware that beauty does not exist in isolation; beauty only manifests itself in brief glimpses or enters into a relationship with the chaotic, the fragmented, the disharmonious etc., which of course are all part of everyday life. "My" angel is punctured, it has a whole, it represents disappointments, disillusion etc. When a child is brought up with fairy-tales, reality is unpredictable and shocking. Both physical and mental pain are actual facts everyone has to deal with. *When An Angel Breaks Her Silence* talks about this insight in different stages from childhood to adult, and of course the title signals that the pain is transformed into written language.

For a young woman it seems a remarkably confident book both in the subject

matter and the rhythm in which it is expressed. Is this actually so?
I had no plan when I wrote *When An Angel Breaks Her Silence*. I didn't doubt. I wrote from urgent necessary – and I still write for the same reason. The rhythm was just there as well as the theme. Often you'll find the key to the rest of a writer's books in the first work, even if refinement of style is not very developed. I still don't have a plan, but I have a sense of what kind of book I'm writing earlier in the process, or at least I find out earlier than before. I remember that when I wrote *Queen's Gate* I had the composition of the whole by the time I wrote the seventh poem, 'Marriage'. Suddenly I knew that I had to write poems about water in all its forms: the drop, the lake, the river, the well, the sea, vital liquids, the bath, the rain and the rainbow.

When An Angel Breaks Her Silence *was published just after the rise of feminist poetry in the seventies. Was your book a reaction to this? Did the feminist movement have any impact upon Pia Tafdrup in her twenties?*
Because of the debates about sexual liberty etc. in the Seventies, I have insisted on living emancipated – with all the crucial problems a free life brings. During the seventies many important social themes were discussed in literature in Denmark, often in essay writing or in a journalistic prose; while my writing was more existentially-oriented right from the start. And still is.

In my generation the reaction to these debating books, with the main focus on the content, was of course a style more conscious of aesthetics. In my case a tension between content and aesthetics exists. Aesthetics are above all an individual matter, a personal staging of the script. *In Walking Over Water*, I say:

> Language is not only what is said, but the way in which it is said. Language constantly creates new expressions and new conditions. My poems must conform to character, my aesthetics are my signature. The successful poem, the one that emerges in all its perfection, will be pondered again and again. On the basis of its aesthetics.

So the "reaction" against many women's writing during the Seventies was for me first of all linguistic condensation. I didn't want to write *about* something: the poem's form should at the same time *show* the content. For example, a poem that expresses desire must demonstrate it in the choice of words, of course, and all the way into the sentence construction. The body must interpose itself as form and the poem develop a syntax of desire. While a poem that depicts snow must have a completely different, muffled construction. The poem must render concrete and sensuous; not postulate or present abstract explanations. The poem's being must be realized in its figure. I find that poetry has a unique linguistic possibility to *be* what is being spoken about.

You rapidly followed your first book with No Hold *(1982), which was influenced by Ludvig Feilberg's philosophy.*

When my first book was published the next was already written, so I never had problems with the second book, which is often regarded as the one that's difficult to write. I was completely absorbed because, during my work on the first book, I'd realized I could not only write poems from my experiences but invent a new universe when I wrote. A suite of twelve poems in *No Hold* is the best example. These poems have an erotic character but they don't refer to a special story in my life. The poems are conglomerates of dreams, longing, fantasy and physical experiences at the same time. I felt an immense freedom writing poems not directly from my own life. These poems deal with Ludvig Feilberg who distinguishes between what you get hold of (*fang*) and what you do not hold or grab (*intetfang*). Feilberg is very wise when it comes to descriptions of meditative and psychological states of mind. We still study Feilberg in Denmark: recently Margit Hartyani published a book on his work.

Is there a different use of language between When An Angel Breaks Her Silence *and the later books?*

For me, poetry has always been a matter of concentration – both in the short and in the longer poem. Poetry is fundamentally different from other genres: quite simply a language within language, where the crystals ripple close to one another. Poetry's density of meaning is not a desire to block out interpretation, but an attempt to open, in concise and pregnant expressions, the manifold quality of thought and imagination. Poems don't just do research. They also construct a universe, an aesthetic world of images. The good poem should be both music and sensuousness – and at the same time carry forth an idea. The words must do it. They must do what they say, the mood must be cultivated, the expression must be as distinct as possible, and yet the text must have a resistance built into it. It is the resistance that determines the leap, what makes the poem attain resilience, mobility and a new insight.

I have had these ideas almost from the very beginning. I still write following them, but *very different* books come out of this. [...] I now have thirteen collections. The latest is *Boomerang* (2008), a hundred and one haiku. When I wrote my first books I began rather minimalistically, with very short and condensed poems. During the late eighties they grew – and in the nineties I built up whole systems. My books from that period all concentrated on a theme: the forest in *The Crystal Forest*, the city in *Territorial Song* – and it's the city of Jerusalem, the book bears the subtitle *A Jerusalem Cycle* – and finally water in *Queen's Gate*. After *Thousandborn* in 1999 (a hundred and one rubaiyat) a new beginning took place. I'm now working on a triad with *The Whales in Paris* and *Tarkovsky's Horses* as the two first books. The third will appear in Denmark in May 2010.

To what extent did the Danish symbolist poet Sophus Claussen influence you?
I have only read Sophus Claussen to a certain extent; he is an equilibrist in language. But I will mention the Swedish poet Gunnar Ekelöf, whose poems I always take with me when I travel and whom I've read for many years, with the same interest and pleasure every time!

[...] Are you always seeking to push the boundaries? How far is technical expertise a guiding principle?
I have the feeling each time that I begin from scratch... When the brain works, it builds on advanced networks and integrated principles. My view of language is that it is "thousand born". The figure of a thousand is magical and fabular. It is associated with the *Thousand and One Nights*, with something that is thousand-fold; but first and foremost I connect the concept of "thousand born" with the process of genesis, with the arrival of words, with thoughts that can unfold themselves in their thousands. As someone who writes, I'm captivated by the thousands of possibilities offered by language. My choice – or its choice of me – has a background that is inscrutable and reaches through the whole of my life. When a poem is written, something is put into the world that was not there before. The words are born out of my mouth or my pen. A large number of alphabets in the world consist of fewer than thirty characters: from these thousands upon thousands of possibilities are born. It is the wonderful assumption of multiplicity that we have in common. And precisely this causes the conditions of Babel.

When I first wrote I was satisfied with a few good lines. For each book I call for more and more from myself, so I don't "control" anything. Sometimes a subject starts the poem, other times a rhythm, or something else. I never know.

In 1991 you published Walking Over Water, *a statement of your poetics. It would be foolish to attempt to summarise it here but nevertheless could you perhaps give an insight into it.*

One passage stands, in a way, as a miniature *Walking Over Water*. I allow myself to quote it here in Anne Born's translation:

> My theory of poetry can be said to be a floating theory of poetry, as all meaning comes from within. Reality is merely reality. What gives it depth and dimension is the accession to it. External reality thus depends on the internal, the emotional. By floating, I am thinking neither of a seraphic position nor of escapism, but of the happy boost which the weight and force of images can produce, the momentary clarity a poem can produce.

Art must be more than merely likeable, the presence of passion is a necessity. To write poems is for me a process that raises and opens and gives me a sense of walking on the water. And thanks to its artifice, a poem will perhaps also make the reader float for a moment.

I hope to link words together in such a way that they receive an aura of significance. The fact that significance comes from inside, and that things must always be motivated in me personally, implies loneliness. But no-one else can produce my insight, just as there are a whole lot of biological conditions which are necessarily mine and mine alone. No one else can awaken from my sleep, no one else can die my death. I belong to myself. I bear my fate. To be alone with himself is something that hardly any human being can stand. But the further I penetrate into loneliness, the less alone I am.

In 1998 you published Queen's Gate, *which was awarded Scandinavia's most prestigious literary award, The Nordic Council Literature Prize, and also the Nordic Prize from the Swedish Academy. To what extent do you see yourself as a Scandinavian writer rather than simply a Danish one?*
I am a poet born in Denmark and my mother tongue is Danish. In that way I am a Danish poet. But when I regard the Nordic countries from, for example, South Europe I feel I have a Nordic identity, and in further distant parts of the world I feel my European roots! [...]

In January, Tarkovsky's Horses *was published here in the UK. What was the inspiration for the book?*
In fact, Bloodaxe are publishing two books in one volume translated by David McDuff. Or perhaps, more accurately, he recreated them. The first book, published in Denmark 2002, is *The Whales in Paris*, which I regard as positing a clash between society and nature. Paris is an important cultural city in Europe, as the whale is a great mammal. You can say that French

philosophy is a whale too. French language and literature have had a very special status in Europe (at least for a decade). I see whales as huge forces of nature. So in that way whales present both nature and culture. *The Whales in Paris* suggests that life can be viewed as a confrontation with what's larger than one's self: love, desire and death – forces that are at play even in modern civilization. *The Whales in Paris* has these big forces in life as a theme but also the suffering we inflict on others, loss, despair and pain.

The second book published in Denmark 2006 is *Tarkovsky's Horses*. The poems here are about my father's last years with dementia – as well as his death. It's certainly not an ideal book to write about your dying father, not when your father has been so incredible. But the book wanted to be written. You can say that it depicts loss in two ways. The poems portray my father's increasing forgetfulness, his loss of everyday skills; in part, they portray the loss of a father. They also show the course an illness takes from when my father is diagnosed to when he has to move into a nursing home and dies almost a year later. The deconstruction of identity is augmented with use of the myth of Orpheus and Eurydice. These poems about oblivion are located in an odd border region, which also calls forth certain comic and grotesque elements. In any case, the poems narrate the drama it is to be human.

In his prime, my father asked me if I would speak at his funeral when that day arrived. Of course, I pushed the thought away; but when he died, I knew I had to write that speech for him. What I didn't know was that I opened up something much larger. What began as a speech developed into *Tarkovsky's Horses*, most of which was written in Berlin immediately following his death.

You're also a novelist and dramatist as well as a poet. Do these different disciplines complement each other or do they access different parts of the writer Pia Tafdrup?
I'd say that the different genres show different sides of me but I am there all the time. Not everything can be said in a poem, so the subject matter determines the genre. A poet is identified by his or her aesthetic signature, that is to say a special personal characteristic or spiritual fingerprint you'll find no matter whether they write prose, drama or poetry.

How do you see Danish literature in the world?
I think every Danish poet or writer today is lucky because of Hans Christian Andersen, Søren Kierkegaard and Karen Blixen (Isac Dinesen), who are well known over the world. [...] I remember I asked in a Chinese school class

whether they knew Hans Christian Andersen. Many, many hands immediately rose into the air. I was really surprised! Difficulties are always connected with translation, especially when it comes to poetry. Every poet has his or her specific universe. I make my "spiritual signature" when I write. It's this special stamp that can be very difficult to reproduce but when it is, I'm really grateful…

In 1981, the year you published your first collection, the Nordic Women's Literary History group was formed. Have Danish women writers been second-class citizens in comparison to the men? Who are the most influential Danish women writers and what impact have they had on your work?

Inger Christensen, who died recently, was a really great poet. But not so many referred to her when she was alive. She didn't publish new books in her last years, but she has written excellent poetry. Now things have changed, but too late… I knew Inger very well and to me she really did complain that some of her male colleges always were mentioned, quoted etc. She sometimes felt she was overlooked in Denmark, compared to Germany where she was highly esteemed. I always looked forward to a new book by Christensen, since I first read her while studying literature at the University of Copenhagen. Even if she didn't get the attention she ought to have had when she was alive, I guess she will be more read the next many years than any other in her generation. She was an outstanding poet.

Ruth O'Callaghan has been widely translated. She recently received an Arts Council bursary travel to Mongolia; her 'Letter from' that country appears in *PR 99:4*.

Bird Nesting With John Clare

ALISON BRACKENBURY

The Beanfields' Scent

It is light as winds, without coldness,
Fresh waves of sea without salt,
It blows a sweet honey, uncloying,
It is happiness without fault.

Its flowers' tongues ask no taxes,
Though their purple is royal; their white
Is pressed by black so pure
That noon is burned by night.

Who buys a scent called "Beanflowers"?
Its glossy blue of leaf
Buckles, to June's sharp showers.
Best things are free and brief.[1]

This poem of mine was left, briefly, in a free pamphlet in a doctor's waiting room. In return, I received an email from a lady in Swindon, who had always loved the scent of beanflowers, but had never before read a poem in its praise. But of course, I had. It was by John Clare.

"Black eyed and white, and feathered to one's feet / How sweet they smell," Clare wrote, remembering fragrance breathed on "battered footpaths". Searching for the poem again, in my yellowed student copy, I find it in the section marked 'Asylum'. A few pages later, in the final poem, I glimpse the phrase "the sedgy fen".

Biography is a fen. I will try, without being sucked down, to say why I was drawn to Clare on his summer footpath. Clare's path is a legend: the farm labourer who read avidly and achieved brief fame as an English working-class poet. His disreputable grandfather was in fact a Scottish schoolteacher. My mother, also from a rather disreputable, partly Welsh

---

1. Alison Brackenbury, *Singing in the Dark*, Carcanet, 2008.

family, trained in London as a teacher, but came back to her Lincolnshire village to my father. Rebelling against generations of shepherds, he was first a ploughboy, like Clare, then a farm lorry driver.

So I first heard Clare at a village school, in the pattering of his "little trotty wagtail". (I spent my earliest years, as he had, roaming woods, finding nests.) My tiny country grammar school brought me no closer to Clare, but delivered me to Oxford, one of a wave of state school pupils, children of the post-war boom and the Welfare State. The world should have been at our feet. But what kind of world was it?

The Seventies should have been golden. They were grey. As the melon-seed necklaces of the Sixties rotted and *Silent Spring* faded on library shelves, supermarkets opened, cars swept on to motorways and the crop-spraying planes flew over Lincolnshire. England grew richer, but not kinder. Oil, briefly, ran out. Several of the unions discovered suicidal greed. Below the academic horizon Structuralism lurked; below the political horizon, Thatcher. It is striking how many poets, artists and singers ended their own lives in the early Seventies. I came close to being one of them. The last sight which made me want to live was a glimpse of rough-coated ponies in a flooded field.

It was not breakdown which drew me to Clare, though I recognise the weariness of his asylum poems, and I am still struck cold by his cry, "Literature has destroyed my head and brought me where I am". I was ill for a few months. Clare was mad for decades. He thought he was Byron. He did not know his wife. But he continued to write. What drew me to Clare was survival. He kept on his paths, in his head. The last poem in my yellowed book has its own light:

> But warm the sun shines by the little wood
> Where the old cow at her leisure chews her cud.

No one else I knew at college read Clare. I found him for myself, in the corners of the Oxford bookshops: new editions, which I would have found nowhere else. We were, perhaps, spoilt children; we were allowed to write about any author we chose. So I wrote about Clare and his "essential imagination", his eye for the small, his ear for its song. I was captivated by a collection Clare made but was never able to publish in his lifetime, which he called 'Bird Nesting'. The poem which stayed with me, muttered and cherished, is one which Clare copied out, in one swift unpunctuated flow. 'The Cuckoo' ends:

When summer from the forest starts
Its melody with silence lies
And, like a bird from foreign parts
It cannot sing for all it tries
'Cuck cuck' it cries and mocking boys
Crie 'Cuck' and then it stutters more
Till quick forgot its own sweet voice
It seems to know itself no more.[2]

Is there a sadder end to a poem? Yet it is light as dance. What is the "essential imagination"? It is the red inside a cuckoo's beak. Clare's work reminded me that the poetry which sustained me drew on years of knowledge, from a world outside books. In the music of the shortening lines are the ballads which Clare's parents sang, which Clare wrote down. Is there, too, the lilt of Burns? Clare, I believe, was shocked to discover that Burns's songs cheerfully stole ballad lines. But perhaps it emboldened him to do so. The close of this poem made me bolder to throw the rules of English syntax into the air, and trust they might come down in the rhythm of a poem. When Clare wrote "quick forgot its own sweet voice" he found his own, most truly.

I could – perhaps – have written a thesis on Clare. I could have become an academic, with the prestige my teachers longed for and the money my parents thought would secure escape from small rooms and hard manual labour. Instead, as *Poetry Review* noted twenty years later, I pulled aside from my Oxford generation and went my "own way". I snatched a First, married, flew.

Clare went with me. I wrote my first book in my twenties, in the time I gained by doing unglamorous, fairly undemanding jobs. Its love poems owed much to the green grass and lost girls of his many songs. My second book had a long poem about Clare called 'Breaking Ground'. It is a poem so close to me that I still cannot judge it. At times I dismiss it, jokingly, and then am humbled when a reader tells me how much it moved them. Certainly it was a poem of passage: from rambling longer pieces (which Clare himself wrote) to a terser, briefer style. I think it lived best in a tumbling ballad. There Clare dreamed of himself as a famous dead boxer, as the villagers cast flowers on his bare coffin:

marigolds of sun and flame
light stocks as sweet as women's love
briar roses, frail as wrists of girls,
with every thorn plucked off[3]

---

2. John Clare, 'Birds Nest', Mid Northumberland Arts Group 1973.
3. Alison Brackenbury, *Selected Poems*, Carcanet, 1992.

'Breaking Ground' was published in 1984. During the 1980s, as I struggled to bring up a child in the jungle of Thatcher's Britain, I began to pay the price of going my own way. Like most people, we lived in a town, in a small shabby Sixties semi, perched next to the trees and foxes by the railway. But I had secured a lifeline to the country. I paid for the lessons my parents could never afford and, an erratic but determined rider, I kept a series of unaffordable horses on the hills: not hunters or thoroughbreds, but rough-coated ponies like those I had glimpsed on Oxford's Port Meadow, or like Flash, whom my grandfather drove in his shepherding cart.

At Oxford, I found gender less of a problem than class. Now both turned against me. A few slim books proved poor repayment for my parents' lavish hopes. Where were the big cool house and the Professorship? Instead they found a Welsh cob, muddy boots, and a possibly neglected child. I had, in any case, reached for the wrong half of my inheritance. The animals were the men's world. Women kept house, immaculately. I then took a manual job in my husband's family business, and, happy in boiler suit and boots, dropped off the social scale.

My own family raged at me. My husband's undermined me. During a decade knotted with family problems, someone remarked to me that they thought most women they knew would have retired from my life to concentrate on a nervous breakdown. But I had Clare's country patience, and I could write.

I discovered recently that Clare knew a ballad about the "Wantley Dragon", which, in the song's last line "groans" and "dies".[4] I was startled by the realisation that the couplets I had always thought he drew from his reading were everywhere in the ballad tradition. I had emerged from school writing staccato free verse; from university, briefly seduced by ambiguity and alternative endings. It took me a long time to rediscover, fully, rhyme, story, ballad. For the last decade, I have poured much of my limited spare time and money into listening intently to folk songs, new and old. My latest book, *Singing in the Dark*, includes a poem called 'Scraper', Clare's name for his fiddle. He was one of the earliest collectors of ballads, and my memory has been enriched by the settings of some of his (unpublished) lyrics by the singer George Deacon:

> I ran with love but was undone.
> O had I walked e'er I did run.[5]

---

4. *George Deacon, John Clare and the Folk Tradition*, Francis Boutle, 1983.
5. *ibid.*

But where does Clare stand as a poet today? It was suggested to me recently that Clare's work is well-known. Some readers of poetry do indeed know his poems very thoroughly. Others do not know them at all, and have no intention of seeking them out, as recent comments in a *Guardian* forum made clear.

I cannot ignore this debate, not just because of my particular tenderness towards Clare, but because it goes to the heart of my own work and life. The English attitude to the countryside, animals, all that is not human, is complicated by a history which involves a constant sweeping of people from the land, notably *via* enclosure and the Industrial Revolution. (Both sides of my family lost farms in the nineteenth century.) But many of the landless English, like me, stubbornly return. They walk, they trespass, they watch birds, they camp in Glastonbury's summer mud.

Criticism of literature, including poetry, seems to me curiously aloof from these stubborn passions. It still seems based in a few major urban and academic centres. Or, by some accounts, just in one. "London is everything" an authoritative guest told me firmly at one of the grander literary parties I have ventured into. Those parties! There is a nineteenth century painting of the great and good talking animatedly of literature, and a shadowy figure, thought to be Clare, staring in fascination at a clock. I have stared at a few clocks. During the darker days of the 1980s, a reviewer of my poems in a major London journal wondered, politely, if there was really any point in writing about birds?

The countryside, wildlife and farming did not mysteriously disappear in 1914, as headlines remind us: 'BSE'. 'FOOT AND MOUTH'. 'SWINE FLU'. It seems likely that we have come close to wrecking the planet, at least as a home for us. With my country obsession with weather, I have been convinced of this since I sat down on my own front doorstep, in the early Nineties, overcome by heat. "It's gone", I thought. "It" is the rich web, of birds, soils, air, plants, seasons, which we have been tearing apart. If we are to repair any of the damage – and we have very little time – it will need drastic action; disruptive change to the comforts which have silted around many of us in England since those grey selfish Seventies. We need to understand, with ear as well as eye, heart as well as head, what we are trying, so late, to save.

John Clare, the shadow who watched the clock, wrote a book which for much of my lifetime has itself existed as a shadow. *The Shepherd's Calendar* has always been a puzzling poem to me. Despite occasional riches, like an old-fashioned 'plum pudding', its monthly accounts of farm, birds and village seemed strangely bare and truncated. Now a new edition, edited by

Tim Chilcott and published by Carcanet in 2006, has been as great a revelation as the exquisite bird poems which I fell upon in the bookshops of the Seventies. For the new edition has Clare's far longer poem, as he sent it to his publishers. It is a tumbling unpunctuated rush, quick as his consciousness, rich as his world. It is completely readable. If you can stumble through 'The Waste Land', you can gallop *The Shepherd's Calendar*. Its appeal is not confined to the relatively few who now live in the English countryside (where the cuckoo, increasingly, fails to return). Unlike Clare's villagers, dispossessed by enclosure, many of us now own small plots of land: gardens, which have increasingly been paved, tarmaced and built on. We are leaving no room for the web of life, the flies, the frogs, the cricket who chirrups all night in my tiny patch by the railway, for Clare's February bee, "which strokes its legs upon its wing".

Clare knew that the great depends on the small. In 'The Shepherd's Calendar', he has an exact, minute account of a hedgehog before his great storm scene. His editor, desperate to mould Clare to London's taste, replaced it with a vaguer verse about sunbeams. His efforts were in vain. The poem was remaindered, and disappeared for over a century. At last, we can hear Clare's words, where the small sweeps into the great, icicles become comets and we, like the shepherd, are left "croodling",[6] hunched beneath the fury of the weather. When I want to find, once more, my place in a world of vast forces, I do not turn to *The New Scientist*, *The Independent*, even to the Bible. I go up to the hills. Or I put down my folder of poems, weave past cats and saddles, and from my already battered copy, I read the end of 'February', from *The Shepherd's Calendar*, by John Clare:

> Nature soon sickens of her joys
> And all is sad and dumb again
> Save merry shouts of sliding boys
> About the frozen furrowd plain
> The foddering boy forgets his song
> And silent goes wi folded arms
> And croodling shepherds bend along
> Crouching to the whizzing storms.[7]

A version of this essay, produced by Julian May, was broadcast on Radio 3 in December 2008.

---

6. 'Croodling', means to hunch from the cold.
7. John Clare, *The Shepherd's Calendar*, edited by Tim Chilcott, Carcanet, 2006.

Iceland Now

RESEARCHED AND INTRODUCED BY JASON RANON URI ROTSTEIN

from *An Interview With Sjón*

Sjón (b. 1962) published his first poetry collection, *Sínir (Visions)*, at fifteen. He was one of the founding members of the neo-surrealist group Medúsa and has published numerous poetry collections and eight novels, as well as writing plays, libretti and picture books for children. His long-time collaboration with the Icelandic singer Björk led to an Oscar nomination for his lyrics for the Lars von Trier movie *Dancer in the Dark* (2000). Together they wrote the opening song for the 2004 Athens Olympics. His latest collection *söngur steinasafnarans* (*the song of the stone collector*) was nominated for the Icelandic Literary Prize in 2007. In 2005 he won the Nordic Council's Literary Prize for his novel *Skugga-Baldur* (*The Blue Fox*), which was long-listed for the 2009 Independent Foreign Fiction Prize. In 2007/08 Sjón was Samuel Fischer Guest Professor at the Freie Universität in Berlin.

JRUR: Where are the intellectuals today in Iceland and what is the specific intellectual need in the community?

Well, I just wonder if there has ever been a real position for the intellectuals in Icelandic society. Traditionally, we are a society where everybody has the right to voice his or her opinion about whatever is happening here. And it doesn't matter if you come from the academe or if you come from the arts, if you are the foreman of the plumber's union, or if you are simply a disgruntled or unhappy bank clerk somewhere, everybody has access to the dialogue through the newspapers. I think this makes the situation here a little bit different from what you can expect in other countries. I mean, most of the voices you see in newspapers, for example, are the so-called ordinary people, the laymen; and, I think, for me this is a very healthy situation. Of course, we have the tradition from the forties and fifties of some key intellectuals, key writers, taking part in social discourse, and, mainly, Halldór Laxness. Earlier on and then in the Seventies you had some [people], especially writers from the left-side, voicing their opinions about this and that and trying to influence the discussion. So I think it's a tricky thing to approach. And I think Icelandic writers, for example, are quite weary of how they should position themselves in the discussion; because most writers I think really don't feel that their voice should have any bigger status than the voice of the cleaning woman who feels the urge to write to the newspapers about the latest legislation in the parliament. So for me that is the landscape, you know. And I personally took very early on a stance against stepping into the social discussion because I really feel that if writers want to have an impact they should do it through their writings and with the tools of literature. And I sincerely believe that the minute a writer writes a piece for the newspaper he has ceased to use the tools of literature – even though he spices it with poetry and funny or clever metaphors and witty irony – or whatever he uses. In most cases, I would say in 99% of the cases, the writer has ceased to be a literary writer and has become some sort of a social analyst or a journalist or whatever. So right from the beginning my position has been to express my ideas about how the society should function, and where the society should go and what should be the basic moral elements of the society; from the beginning, I've only wanted to do this through my writing.

So nothing has changed really since the crash for you in terms of your writing? Do you notice a change in your writing? Do you see yourself even obliquely dealing with some of the issues at stake?
I obviously know that this will find its way into what I write. But I also feel that I have, let's say for the last ten, twelve, fifteen years, been writing about the elements that brought this crash on. And I think for most writers they have already been dealing with those elements in society and in our psychological makeup, in the psychological makeup, of the people living here. [...]

But having said all that, also, I've never understood why writers answer to the call of politicians and academics – *to do this and that*. And obviously after the crash there has been a lot of demand that writers do this and that. "Oh now we the writers should write to the newspapers, now the writers should deal with this in their poems. Now the writers should do this and that..." I've always completely hated this idea of the writers doing this and that. Writers should be exploring society through literary tools and thereby exploring also the tools of literature. But having said all that, it is obvious that this discussion about what has happened is already taking place in the theatre. And it seems that the theatre has responded quite fast, and I would say efficiently and effectively, to what is happening. Actually I have just finished a play that will be premiered in the beginning of February. [...]

A year ago I was approached by a director here called Rúnar Guïbrandsson who has a theatre group called Lab Loki, which comes from the direction of experimental, challenging physical theatre. He is really I think one of the most interesting theatre directors here. And he called me a year ago just after the crash happened, and commissioned a play. Because I have never written anything directly into a social situation, I thought, okay, maybe this is my chance to do it. I knew instantly that I was taking the chance of failing spectacularly. Maybe I will. I will know in the beginning of February if I have failed spectacularly. I really in a way feel very comfortable to do this in the theatre, because the theatre is a place where you can have a more direct dialogue than you can in poetry or in the novel. You can shout slogans from the stage. It is a platform. It is something close to the meeting, it is close to the live meeting. So it is already one step closer to the place where a discourse really happens in society. It has been quite a challenge. The play is not obviously political. But at the same time no one will be in doubt about where it's coming from.

Do you feel pressure to make your work accessible because of the milieu of the layman writing for a newspaper or people feeling as if the intellectual has to come off his high horse and meet the people half way?
Well, I've been asked to, what I would call, water my work down from the beginning. In a way my generation, I was born in 1962, we have from beginning been perceived as quite elitist and arrogant and unaware of the needs of the layman. But I think that's such a big part of the writer's job – such a big part of the writer's job is to be difficult and is to work with the most complicated tools of language...

The widest yardstick.
...Yes. Come on, everybody else can do that other thing and they are doing it all the time. But I think in Iceland we have a quite long-standing respect for writers and for literature. And I don't think people here would like writers to become populist and to water themselves down. I think they like us to be as artistic and difficult as possible. And they know that they will have to take a step towards us. But of course, every writer wants to have a reader. You never make your work so complicated that you only have three readers – yourself, your editor and your wife. [...]

Do you think that the best writers still make it to the top of the heap?
Yeah, yeah, and I think there are enough people here who recognize talent, where talent lies. So I've got no problem with that. I really think this democratic way of doing things has helped us discover talent that usually would not or otherwise find its way into the centre of the literary scene here. But what I think is important in Icelandic literature now, what I think is

important for Icelandic society, is that we find a way of opening up, to make it easier for those who never before have had a voice in Icelandic literature – and that is the immigrants, that is foreigners that have come to stay here. At the moment the literary scene is absolutely closed to them. There are no places where they can approach the publishing houses. Because you would have to read it in Polish and then you would have to translate it. Are you going to wait for the poor Polish writer to get enough command of Icelandic to start writing? For me it has been obvious for quite some years now that the next big step for literature is when those voices are going to be heard. And I think that's much more important than how Icelandic born and bred writers will respond to this crash. Because this crash is not going to be our September 11th. This is of course a big moral shock. But for people who have really been looking at the society for years this isn't such a shock. […]

But what about the purity of the language? Icelandic is known for not accepting loan words. What do you think would happen in terms of that? Do you think that the language would go through a renovation as well?
I'm sure that will be. I don't know. I tend to look at this from a distance: this language is going to be changing anyway and I think it would be much more rewarding *for* the language if it happens in a way where we embrace the changes that the immigrant writers, the possibility immigrant writers, will bring. Then we are actually encouraging someone to actually write about his experience of being here, translating it into words, filtering it through his Thai, or Polish, or whatever his language and experience. That is a dynamic way for the language to change. And the language will change. It's not like it's ever been possible to keep a language pure. The Icelandic written language in the eighteenth century was so full of Danish and German that to read official letters at the time was really... They really look bad to us today.

Let's just get back to the question of politics for a minute. I'm interested to know what place you see for politics within in poetry; whether you think that poetry can ever be devoid of politics? This is an ongoing question.
I don't think poetry should be devoid of politics. And I think poetry has never really been devoid of politics. Poetry is always so much about the individual's experience. So it has to, it has to, *it has to* deliver the individual's experience of whatever political situation there is. [...]

And your influences..?
In the beginning I was simply influenced by the Icelandic Atom Poets. But

when I started looking at where their influences came from it was obvious that they were very much influenced by the Surrealist tradition. So that's where I went as well. And in the Eighties we had this little surrealist group here called Medusa and we were exploring the possibilities of surrealism. But what we did, which the Atom Poets did not, was that we mixed it with a more outgoing agenda. Because we were also influenced by punk. For us, it was the combination of the do-it-yourself attitude of punk, and surrealism. So right from the beginning it was very much about bringing the message out there. So we were reading at the punk concerts. You usually had surrealist poets between bands trying to break down the barriers between the real and the imaginary. Which was quite a challenge for us the poets, because at those gigs nobody was there for the poetry. Absolutely nobody was there for the poetry, nobody came for the surrealist poets, they all came for the music. And then you went on stage and you really had to tough it out for your fifteen minutes. You really had to find a way of delivering it, so they wouldn't just boo you off the stage in the first minute. So for us from the beginning it was a mixture of a social agenda mixed with a really true and strong belief in the revolutionary possibilities of poetry. We really believed that things would change with surrealist poetry. We really believed that creating all those weird little things would have an impact. And I think we did in a way. I think we managed to do quite a lot. I don't think we changed society. But we managed to introduce much more aggressive *avant garde*-ist approach to poetry and the arts.

Do you think there is a collective like that nowadays? Do you think that your group in any way aligned with music?
For us it was so much also about dialogue and collaboration between art forms. As you probably know, there were two published poets in the Sugarcubes, the bass player and the guitarist, both of them had published two or three books of poetry and were recognized poets, young poets, at the time. So right from the beginning for us it came absolutely easy together and from the beginning we completely rejected the idea of "high art" and "low art." I saw no difference between writing poetry to be published in books and to be read on the stage and let's say Einar Örn, the singer in the Sugarcubes, making his lyrics and bringing them to people through his music. I never thought his was a lesser art. Or he never thought, Oh he is working in the snobbish arts. So from the beginning we saw no barriers and no difference. It was just you and your friends expressing yourself through different means. And I think that was something new here. […]

How do you compare Icelandic literature with other Scandinavian literatures? How has that relationship changed from the way it was in the past?
As far as I know, I think we are actually doing quite well. I think, for example, the Danes have had an incredibly strong and great poetry scene. For the last twenty years I would say, maybe twenty-five years, since the beginning of the eighties. I actually think the Danes are better poets than Icelanders. I think you see such strong and beautifully made poetry there.

And why do you think that is?
I think they've nurtured their poets very well. I mean in 86/87 they founded this Writer's School there. Do you know this?

No...
It's an incredible little idea... There was a Danish poet and critic called Poul Borum and he was really always looking for the new, new things. And in the late Eighties, he founded this Writer's School. It's a creative writing school but founded by writers and completely built on the writer's experience.

Do they study classical texts?
It's mostly focused on creating new texts. Of course they get some background and they get some literary history but it's mostly about…

There has been a lot of criticism and backlash against some of the writer's workshops in the US and in England: but you think that this worked well?
This has been really working so well in Denmark. It's really been an incredible breeding place for young talent. So I really think they've been nurturing their young poets there. Here in Iceland to be a young poet is really just a struggle. As you know most young poets here begin by self-publishing. That's how we all begin really. You publish your things yourself. And fortunately because of how small the country is you manage, even though you might publish yourself, one or two reviews in the papers. And pretty soon after your first book you might find yourself at a reading where you are reading with more established poets. […]

[But] I was definitely very aware when I wrote *The Blue Fox* that I was writing a very Nordic book. A book really feeding on the North, on Nordic society and the social values of our society. The common values that the Nordic society has: its stance towards the weak, and the meek and how they are positioned in society, and the possibility of redemption through the position you take towards the meek. […]

There is something about people like [Octavio] Paz and [Odysseus] Elytis which I admire and envy. And that is the incredibly broad vision they have. They somehow manage to write about the universe and the life of the ladybird in the same poem. And this is something I think is also important for today; poetry should still be the platform in which we can still have this broad vision, which can position man in the big picture, especially now when we have this huge comeback of religion, and religion is again claiming its role as the tool to position man. Then I think poetry should really state its case again as the other great tool we have, the tool that is devoid of dogma, the tool that is the humanist way of positioning man. [...]

Clearly people, writers, have been moving away from the country, maybe what you would call the native realm, and moving to the cities. Could you see a person like Halldór Laxness flowering today? He was more in touch I think with the land than a lot of writers today are. Maybe that's wrong.
Let's say the fairy tale that was Halldór Laxness will not repeat itself in the way it happened then, because the incredible thing about Halldór Laxness is his literature. He is actually born in Reykjavik. So this is a man who is born in a town of ten thousand people. And he manages to find a way of holding the medal of the Nobel Prize in his hand one day. And for me that is an example of how literature should work. I am sure there is a town of ten thousand people in Benin today. It's just possible that a Nobel Prize winner is taking his first steps there now. That is the magical thing about literature: that it belongs to everyone. Storytelling belongs to everyone. Poetry belongs to everyone.

So that particular story will not repeat itself. But I think we still have the situation here where writers, even though they are born and bred in Reykjavik – as I am you know – have contact with the country and the past. On the other hand, it is a question of whether the country has anything to tell us – and we should be challenging and channelling that. I'm not sure, but I think this democratic thing that I was talking about earlier – how we welcome new writers – is really the key to how Icelandic literature can renew itself and why I think it keeps being interesting.

Hotel Holt, Reykjavík, 27 November 2009.

Jason Ranon Uri Rotstein is a Visiting Fulbright Scholar and an Icelandic Ministry of Culture Scholar at the University of Iceland, Reykjavík.

Sjón
(from the book of illusions)

reykjavík 11.03.'80

dear f.

last night I dreamed you cut
all your hair off and used it to make a bed in which we
made love, on the facing wall was a mirror
and when I came I saw in
it that you were no longer with me.
you sat in a chair lacquering your fingernails
with green nail polish made out of grasshoppers.
     you said: red houses are your wives.
then I woke up because I had bit myself in the
shoulder. it was half past six.
     otherwise everything is fine, it is
cold here but warm enough for an old
tiger.

     bye, your friend
            sigurjón

Translated by David McDuff

Kári Tulinius
ATLANTSHAFSEKKUR

éghefaðeinsþekkt
hanasemholunasem
samræðurbeygjast
kringumísamk mum
fjölskylduminnar
bringufiðurreitt
burtaffjölskyldu
flagbarðiðhrundi
moldarkófþyrlast
þaðhefurekkisest
ennenmunjáþaðmun
einminningumhana
stjarnaísvarthol
hverfurogmunekki
sleppaójáóekkijá
sjálfsm●rðerhvað

Atlantic Ocean Sinks

I have only known her as the hole that conversation curves around
in family gatherings

Breast-feathers plucked off a family

The eroded hill collapsed a dust cloud swirls it hasn't settled yet
but it will yes it will

One memory of her

A star disappears into a black hole and will not escape oh yes oh
yeah right

Suicide is what

Translated by the author

Kári Tulinius lives in Providence, Rhode Island. His first novel, *Píslarvottar án hæfileika*
(*Martyrs Without Talent*), will be published by Forlagið in May.

Elías Knörr

Two housewives dance on a clothesline
and make love with funambulism
One is a cotton flower
and the other is a silky butterfly
Under the influence of the cleaning
          they write poems on the laundry

*

Blooddrops wake up early in the mirror
many injured eyes appear at home

But let us do flowers out of the morning

The truth is
                    a satirically composed space
it may be decorated with fertility and stars
it may be healed
                    with glowing flowers

          One morning
the girl wakes up in a labyrinth
and bleeds herself blind
She has her home in the mirror pictures

But let us make silence out of the morning
          let us dress the echo in a straitjacket

Translated by the author

Elías Knörr is a young poet. Born into a family of sailors, he's probably the first man in his family never to go to sea. Instead, he decided to study (Icelandic and Italian) philology and move abroad. His first collection, *The Fisherman with the Morning Horses Under the Dress*, appears shortly.

NATIONAL POETRY COMPETITION

*P*oetry Review is glad to continue its annual tradition of publishing the three prize-winning poems from the National Poetry Competition. This year's judges were Daljit Nagra, Ruth Padel and Neil Rollinson.

FIRST PRIZE

Helen Dunmore
The Malarkey

Why did you tell them to be quiet
and sit up straight until you came back?
The malarkey would have led you to them.

You go from one parked car to another
and peer through the misted windows
before checking the registration.

Your pocket bulges. You've bought them sweets
but the mist is on the inside of the windows.
How many children are breathing?

The malarkey's over in the back of the car.
The day is over outside the windows.
No street light has come on.

You fed them cockles soused in vinegar,
you took them on the machines.
You looked away just once.

You looked away just once
as you leaned on the chip-shop counter,
and forty years were gone.

You have been telling them for ever
Stop that malarkey in the back there!
Now they have gone and done it.
Is that mist, or water with breath in it?

Ruth Padel says of Helen Dunmore's 'The Malarkey', "This poem sprang out at me at once, on first read-through, from ten and a half thousand poems, because of the surprising focus it gave, linguistically, imaginatively and emotionally, on something that was not there. It was not showy. I found it completely arresting in its quietness; in the hidden strength of what it was saying so unobtrusively."

SECOND PRIZE

Ian Pindar
Mrs Beltinska In The Bath

Pavel in profile
his eye at the spy-hole
watches Mrs Beltinska in the bath.

Steam from the spy-hole
rises and unravels in the dark
cold apartment at his back,

where a TV with the sound down
shows the River Vltava
bursting its banks.

And as Prague's metro floods
and the Mala Strana floods
and the Waldstein Palace floods

and the National Theatre floods
and the Kampa Modern Art Museum floods,
Mrs Beltinska sinks her treasures in the suds.

The first Czech Bible (1488) is drowned
in sewage water, but the warm orange glow
from Mrs Beltinska's bathroom

coming through the spy-hole
gives an odd kind of halo
to Pavel's head seen from behind.

John Stammers
Mr Punch In Soho

You would recognise that hook nose anywhere,
his hump and paunch, the shiny pink erection of his chin.
Withered, crossed legs on the barstool
dangle like transplants from a much smaller body.
He could have found his ideal slot in the Gestapo,
been a dab hand with a blinding iron.
And the scold's bridle would have been right up his Strasse.
He has, they say, killed seven police:
old-time rozzers on the beat
more deserving of a saucy come-on from the street girls
than the last rites down a back alley.
And two wives. Poor old Mrs Punch finally copped it
one night after he'd done a few dozen barley wines
and as many double gins. She fought fiercely
against *an assailant or assailants unknown*
the Pall Mall Gazette reported. Never caught.
Never charged. And pretty little Mrs Punch
number two won't be taking a bath
in those bubbles again. That's the way to do it!
Just picture him afterwards, cock in hand
like an old chimp with a hard, green-tipped banana.
And the baby, where's the baby?
It's something to make the Devil into the good guy:
how children cry out for him
to drag Punch down to hell for eternal punishment.
But he'd throttle Lucifer when his back was turned
and be back on that stool for closing time.
Or maybe that's where he's been all these years
of grown-up sleep, peaceful and free of nightmare.
It's what you can't see in the stare of his wooden yellow eye.
Don't look, there's his stick, the awful stick!

REVIEWS

[...] if you are aware of God's absence, then
you are aware of God – as of a dead parent.
– Adam Thorpe

Bodies Of Work

STEVEN MATTHEWS

John Burnside, *The Hunt in the Forest*, Cape Poetry,
£10, ISBN 9780224089272;
Ciaran Carson, *On the Night Watch*, Gallery Press,
€13.90, ISBN 9781852354664

John Burnside and Ciaran Carson are both exceptionally prolific writers, who have made their multitudinous productivity integral to that capture of the world which their poetry seeks to make. Burnside's new book is his eleventh poetry collection; he has published seven novels and two volumes of memoir as well. Carson's *For All We Know* appeared only last year, together with a hefty *Collected*; he too is a novelist, and is also a translator. Both these new collections, therefore, further the accumulation of themes and insights, offering sets of variations upon particular worlds.

The philosophical ambition of Burnside's poetry had perhaps been most evident in his last collection. *Gift Songs* opens with a series of 'Responses to Augustine of Hippo', and closes with the immodest 'Four Quartets'. *The Hunt in the Forest* offers us several meditative 'Essays', concerning Light, and Time, as well as other discursive sequences, and several poems carrying the same title, 'Amor Vincit Omnia' (Geoffrey Hill's late work is another shadowing presence here). But the tone has darkened in this new book: one of the most brilliant group of lyrics, 'In Memoriam', charts the terrible slow death of a hospital patient. Other elegies are scattered through the book. In the presence of these specific deaths, Burnside's consistent themes of loss, of alternative selves, of the difficulties of faith, accumulate new power. Governed as they are by a persistent enquiry about the thing-ness of the body, the lyrics of 'In Memoriam' yet celebrate the normal rhythms of gathered experience. "On the surgery ward", the patient restlessly seeks to grasp at a past which is now sadly remote, nearly sealed away for ever, "hoping to catch / the ghost" of:

> ...that no man's land you find
> on the drive to the airport, say, or a Sunday excursion:
>
> a frontier of trees, or a pond at the edge of a meadow
> where something you must have disturbed has hurried aside

and left you a liverish stain in the yellowing grass,
all feathers and teeth, and a tatter of hallelujah.

Syntax and lineation, as always in Burnside, dictate the energy and possibility of the passage, enable it to accumulate the details of the world even as it is moving further away from the patient's consciousness. As ever, those facets are not explored in and for themselves; they remain a set of possibilities from which the patient, and poet, seem curiously disconnected. One lyric from the sequence 'An Essay Concerning Time', 'Konisberg', opens with the line "The places we never visit:", and proceeds precisely to visit some of them, those places set apart from time, including the simultaneous knowledge we have that "no one is truly absent".

The unremitting earnestness of Burnside's enterprise can sometimes become a burden. Too often, the sequences lapse into the near-pretentiousness of a rhetoric about the subject, rather than revealing the marvellous potential in the subject itself. But in the elegies, and in the lyrics about aging – the moving 'Old Man, Swimming' closes the book – there are wonderful gains here upon new territory, together with the persistent, cumulative, concerns of Burnside's previous work.

Carson's *On the Night Watch* sees him, too, underpinning the energies of the book with a by-now-familiar numbers game. We are presented with sonnets gathered in three forty-two poem 'Movements' – a perfectly ratio-ed whole. The book is formally, as in other ways, a homage to its dedicatee, Seamus Heaney. For these are sonnets containing very short lines, so combining two forms which Heaney has mastered; the blank verse fourteen-liner, and the slim, arterial forms of the poetry of the *North* era. Some poems' last lines also serve as titles for later ones, enhancing the sense of cumulative interconnectedness which centres the book.

Carson wrote an intelligently sceptical review of the fatalistic implications of *North* when it first appeared, and this new book stands its ground against some of Heaney's continuing presumptions. Where Heaney had famously dug down into the turf to bring out the victims of perennial violence, Carson's work here, post-Troubles, seems more anxious to let things rest. As 'This Field of Eyebright' puts it: "what the coulter / turned up // beside sod / the shards // & hoards / of bones // we ploughed back / into the soil."

Ironically, though, such ploughing back leads to its own sense of defeat for Carson; in 'The Pit', we hear that "for years I have / been digging so // to find myself / no further on". As with his previous work, surveillance of the self, between lovers, in society, and through history, confines the writing – 'In whose eyes', as the non-rhetorical question of one sonnet title has it. The concern is that, in an aging and ailing body (part of the surveillance described in the poems is medical), the potential for vision itself becomes damaged. Some of the most violent and striking imagery here concerns eyes, as do some of the most beautiful and salving. Faced by a "blip" on the scanner screen, the speaker is left to ask

> exactly what
>
> it was I saw
> a shaft of light
>
> an arrow
> driven through
>
> the eye-slit
> of a helmet

Against such premeditative violences, the flittering recurrence of the flower eyebright, a salve against weakened eyesight, proffers a more positive, romantic, possibility. This is particularly so in the last several sonnets, where memory is linked, as a female, and a lover's, presence, to "eyesight / flowering", a recovery of insight that is also haunted by its dark opposite, since "to forget is / a common verb". Carson is gambling a lot here with the formal riskiness driving the book, and it does not always work. Sometimes the vocabulary is not varied or vivid enough to withstand the vulnerability and exposure conferred upon it by the short lines. But at other points, the writing attains a true Heaneyesque mimeticism in its ambition to deploy its form to speak "of all I have // forgotten / thence to plumb // what was immeasurable".

Steven Matthews is Professor of Poetry at Oxford Brookes University; his essay *Modern Poetry: A Way Of Happening Or Of Non-Happening* appeared in *PR 99:3*.

Fiction As Autobiography

DOUGLAS HOUSTON

Bernardine Evaristo, *Lara*, Bloodaxe Books, £8.95, ISBN 9781852248314;
Arto Vaun, *Capillarity*, Carcanet Press, £9.95, ISBN 9781857549911;
Thomas McCarthy, *The Last Geraldine Officer*, Anvil,
£10.95, ISBN 9780856464218;
Alan Brownjohn, *Ludbrooke: An Introduction*, The Poetry Trust,
£5, ISBN 9780955091020

Bernardine Evaristo's semi-autobiographical *Lara* covers five generations, with vivid tracings of the Nigerian, British, Brazilian, Irish, and German components of her family background. These provide the map for the journeys between Europe, Africa, and South America that complete Lara's quest for identity.

A discipline of single-page verse paragraphs is imposed on the poetic units making up her twenty chapters, a technique that contributes to the narrative's clarity and pace. These verse paragraphs invariably effect a lyrical and emotional closure that makes them entirely adequate to standing alone as poems, even when they deal with such unpromising materials as bigotry directed against the courtship of Lara's Nigerian father and British mother:

> Slut! Look at her trotting along without a care,
>
> who does she think she is, Lady Bleedin' Docker?
> For the love of God someone help her see the light.

The book's documentary textures offer a close-focus social history of prejudice: which does not discriminate between Irish, German, or African targets. *Lara* remains, however, a fundamentally affirmative testimony to identity and antecedents and sings its celebratory qualities in occasional poems of finely judged erotic candour and lyrics of equatorial exoticism.

A preliminary note defines the "capillarity" of Arto Vaun's title as "The interaction between contacting surfaces of a liquid and a solid that distorts the liquid surface". This phenomenon provides an overarching metaphor for tensions between social determinism and the necessary fluidity of evolving personal identity. Vaun's familial sense of displacement includes a feeling of thin-rootedness in the America of his birth as the son of Armenian expatriates. The modern history of Armenia, with its scars of genocide and oppressions, is an understated presence that haunts the book through an inherited sense of insecurity and persecution. Vaun doggedly avoids the full stop throughout the sixty-six numbered but untitled poems, but uses the upper-case convention at line openings to emphasise the linear thrusts by which his work proceeds:

> Let them come forward, who have been nudged off the map
> Let them come forward, who have forgiven and cry while driving
> Let them come forward, who smell the cut grass and the wound
> around the corner
> Let them come forward, who are my kin, your kin, and there when
> our hands sweat

These lines are from the opening poem, whose first line – "America, now I will try it this way" – takes up the Whitmanesque vocative Vaun uses repeatedly to address the matter of America, which is also invoked in his echo of Emma Lazarus's "Give me your tired, your poor, / Your huddled masses […]". The urgent incompatibility of USA's idealistic rubric and the dumbed-down realities of The Great Society begs the question of "Who will speak in tongues to rattle the coma of this land". Vaun's poems are pervaded by a passionate intelligence that is at once both nakedly personal and socially wide-angle in its views of the past and present.

Thomas McCarthy's *The Last Geraldine Officer* takes its title from Colonel Gerald FitzGerald of the Irish Guards, the protagonist of a one hundred and five-page sequence that follows the gathering of individual poems with which the book opens. These are subtly continuous with FitzGerald's story, evoking as they recurrently do Waterford places known since childhood to McCarthy and subsequently encountered within the sequence. Elsewhere, his poetry of Shanghai, Athens, and London is vibrantly metropolitan and movingly humane, while his reflections on contemporary Irish life have an entertainingly quirky charm.

There simply isn't space to dwell further on the book's first section, with barely enough to do justice to the multi-faceted achievement of the title sequence. Here, McCarthy's faux-autobiographical mode consists of poetry, journal entries from WWII combat zones, and a range of recipes from traditional Waterford cuisine. Each recipe is accompanied by a note indicating its associations for FitzGerald: the idyll of the Big House with its woods, meadows, and river, the privileged order of his Anglo-Irish origins that political upheaval has relegated to memories as limpid as Yeats's of Lissadell:

> [...] Templemaurice House,
> Light in the cool dust of Nineteen Nineteen –
> A grid of morning on the bare floorboards,
> Oak light and ivy, and the lead-crystal green
>
> Of a Waterford demense.

Fluent in *Gaeilge* from boyhood, FitzGerald's dilemma is that of one who honours equally the Irish and English dimensions of his character and feels both are called into question by the Irish Republic's neutrality during WWII. FitzGerald's *Gaeilge* poems are woven into the narrative, but no concessions to the inviolability of the language are made by way of translation. The book's acknowledgements allude to a 1940s edition of the poems of Colonel FitzGerald. The possible disingenousness of this information – neither Google nor the catalogue of the National Library of Ireland offers any support for the existence of the Colonel or his works – only makes the more impressive the imaginative coup McCarthy carries off in bringing FitzGerald and his world so vividly to life.

Alan Brownjohn's new pamphlet introduces us to the urbanely evasive *Ludbrooke* in sixteen poems that offer tangential glimpses of an active, if unsatisfactory, social and amatory life. This is a view from the inside, a survey of morally liminal territory that is at once strictly personal and familiar to all as the habitat of lurking vanities. That Brownjohn creates Ludbrooke from familiar materials is clear from his statement that "I've found somebody fictitious to represent the disagreeable elements in my own character" (Poetry Trust press release). His neurotic concern with appearances gives him little peace:

> [...] friends might say, "Whatever you think of Ludbrooke,
> He has his own kind of 'dash', his own 'panache'.
> To be 'devil-may-care' at his age is a talent
> Vouchsafed to a few, you have to envy him."
> Yes, his friends might say that; though he has yet to hear them.

If he is "disagreeable", he keeps it to himself. The worst of his Prufrockian social offences is to let his pen leak onto his host's linen. It seems more of Lubrooke awaits us in Brownjohn's forthcoming *Ludbrooke and*

Others. I look forward to renewing and extending my acquaintance with him.

Douglas Houston is a writer and editor living in Huddersfield. His *New and Selected Poems* is to be published by Shoestring Press this year.

Firecrackers

TARA BERGIN

John Ashbery, *Planisphere*, Carcanet, £12.95, ISBN 978184770899;
Toby Martinez de las Rivas, *Faber New Poets 2*, Faber, £5, ISBN 9780571249961;
Brian Henry, *Quarantine::Contagion*, Arc, £11.99 HB/ £8.99 PB
ISBN 9781906570132/ 9781904614739;
Mahmoud Darwish, *Mural*, trans. Rema Hammami and John Berger,
Verso, £9.99, ISBN-13: 9781844674107

John Ashbery's new collection opens with a question: "Is it possible that spring could be / once more approaching?" Such a beginning not only reveals a poet who has seen many springs, but confirms Ashbery's ability to combine engaging, conversational camaraderie with urgent, fragmented intensity. Spring, he says playfully, is breathy – "you have to say that for it" – but then he shifts skilfully to this clear, visual simile:

> And should further seasons coagulate
> into years, like spilled, dried paint, why,
> who's to say we weren't provident?

In *Planisphere*, Ashbery continues to demonstrate the exciting characteristics of the New York School – the use of popular imagery, surrealistic turns of thought, and high-spirited humour – as well as what has been called his sensitivity to verbal collage. Casually spoken phrases merge with historical flashbacks and inner voices:

Poetry is seriously out of joint.
Fakirs pursue us. Late for the banquet again!
Seriously how can you stand yourself
the way you are well that's the way I am.   ('Variation in the Key of C')

For over thirty years John Ashbery worked as an art critic, and the impact of the visual arts on his writing is well documented. In an interview in 2003, Ashbery said: "I cultivated a quality of paying attention to the art I was supposed to write about so that I could remember when I got home what I had seen." This quality is palpable in *Planisphere*, where Ashbery pays close attention to a whole manner of things, especially to how we use language. His book is an explosive mass of words and thoughts. It's not always possible to find a central thread of meaning within this, and sometimes it feels as if the "poetry dissolves". But this can also become part of the pleasure. As Ashbury says in 'The Winemakers': "Have you considered firecrackers? / The deft music contained therein / assuages all contenders."

Among the four winners of last year's Faber New Poets awards was Toby Martinez de las Rivas, whose pamphlet of twelve poems was published in 2009. One of the most exciting things about this collection is the way it enthusiastically embraces a poetic language which is both descriptive and symbolic: "They have nailed your husband / to the branches of the ragged oak," Rivas writes in 'The White Road', "and the lamb has changed places / with the tiger, nothing is as it was." Many of the poems reveals his appreciation for traditional and oral forms, making effective use of simple repetition, listing, and rhyme: "With a ha ha ha and a ho ho ho, my father brought me round, / My eyes were anchored in the dark, my body to the ground." ('The First Appearance of the Angel of Death, in His Aerial Form'). Regularly, the poems examine their own material, for example in 'Twenty-One Prayers for Weak or Fabulous Things', or 'Things I Have Loved': and it is material with real lyrical power. It's heartening to see it recognised by such a prestigious publisher as Faber and Faber.

Brian Henry is an American poet who has published five collections of poetry. His book-length poem *Quarantine::Contagion*, published by Arc in 2009, was nominated for the Pulitzer Prize and the National Book Award. The book is split into two parts, each consisting of forty short, numbered sections. The second reverses and condenses the first. They begin with the voice of a man who lies in a field beside his wife and son. All three have recently died from the plague. The opening lines, slipping into repetition and using little punctuation, appear to be removing themselves from their own structure, mirroring the separation of the man's spirit from his redundant body: "as I was thinking to keep myself here / where I could not be dead could not be / dead could not be [...]". Expertly, tenderly, and cruelly, sounding at times as if he were translating a Bushmen song-cycle, Brian Henry evokes the horrors of the plague. But there is another isolating pain troubling the narrator. It is portrayed just as cruelly, just as tenderly:

> I left for the river and let a man there
> touch me inside he ripped something
> inside and he told me my scars
> would be beautiful when they healed

The image of the river runs through this volume; it is where the man learns about violence, beauty and death. Appropriately then, the second part becomes a fragmented reflection of the first. A difficult structural move, it is successful in the way it returns to and isolates some of Henry's most striking phrases: "A jagged fire in the mouth and a knot. / The white scarf still in one hand." By the end of the book we are back at the beginning, the final image repeating the first. Henry's song has turned full circle, returning – like the dead narrator – to the earth.

Mural is a new translation by John Berger and Rema Hammami of two late works by Mahmoud Darwish, one of the most acclaimed contemporary poets in the Arab world. Darwish was once described by another of his translators, the young poet Fady Joudah, as "a songmaker whose vocabulary is accessible but whose mystery is not bashful." In the long title poem, written in 2000 after a sudden illness, the poet asks, "Death wait for me Death." The poem is a speech – of both parting and arrival, paying homage to all aspects of life: to language ("deep in the cooing of a dove"); to love ("a storm among trees"); to nature ("This sea is mine / This sea air is mine"); and to the physical body among that natural world ("This quayside with my footsteps and sperm upon it [...] is mine"). Although Darwish's poetry is spiritual and mythical ("I'm lit by Anat's round moon"), there is also evidence in *Mural* of what the poet calls "the ebb of poetry towards prose." Some things he must say plainly: "Now the electronic button works alone / the killer doesn't hear his victims."

'The Dice Player' was Darwish's final poem. Looking over his past, the poet concentrates on the notion of chance, childhood memories illustrating uncertainty: "I feared a lot for my brothers and father / feared for time made of glass / feared for my cat and my rabbit [...]". By the end he asks, "Who am I to defy nothingness? who am I? who am I?" This New Year's Day, John

Berger delivered an 'Alternative Thought for the Day' on Radio Four's *Today* Programme. His subject was Mahmoud Darwish. Darwish's poetry, he said, is "a poetry of resistance. But at the same time – and this is so important – it's a poetry that admits loss, vulnerability, and absolutely refuses political rhetoric."

Tara Bergin is studying for a PhD on Ted Hughes's translations of Pilinszky.

Sacred And Not Profane

ADAM THORPE

Mary Oliver, *Evidence*, Bloodaxe, £8.95, ISBN 9781852248475;
John Glenday, *Grain*, Picador, £8.99 ISBN 9780330461344;
Dorothy Molloy, *Long-Distance Swimmer*, Salmon €12, ISBN 9781907056215;
Fiona Benson, *Faber New Poets 1*, Faber, £5, ISBN 9780571249954

These four poets either believe in God, or believe in His absence, suggesting that if you are aware of God's absence, then you are aware of God – as of a dead parent. "The world is too much with us," as Wordsworth famously complained, craving the "outworn creed" of paganism and its attunement to myth and magic. In Britain, this Romantic urge dwindled through the Georgians and all but finished in the trenches, but in America Transcendentalists like Emerson, Thoreau and Emily Dickinson, and the country's vaster spaces, natural wonders and shamanic indigens, established a perhaps-firmer basis for the spiritual and even mystical tradition in poetry.

Mary Oliver is one of its best-known American practitioners, winning the Pulitzer Prize in 1983. Now in her seventies, her output seems undiminished. She has lived on Cape Cod for most of her life, honouring its resonant "shallows". She has an Emersonian belief in the power of thought to redeem, which gives her verse a sometimes relentless cheeriness – very few British poets admit to being 'happy', after all. But for Oliver beautiful things exist, not to prick us with a sense of loss, but "to excite the viewers toward sublime thought". Her poetry is more transparent wash than sensual oils: in fact, it is all thought. A record of the freshening of her mind as it experiences grass, wind, animals, water, trees, at the same time it craves to give these things significance beyond her own "lonely" relishing.

This is the tension that often makes her simple lines arresting:

> There is the heaven we enter
> through institutional grace
> and there are the yellow finches bathing and singing
> in the lowly puddle.

Is this an ironic comparison? Not really. In the Hermetic, Transcendentalist tradition, with its famous dictum "As above, so below", the unseen simply echoes itself in the visible world. This is what Oliver means, in fact, by her titular "evidence". Her visionary glimpses may borrow here and elsewhere from the lexicon of the Bible – "bathing and singing", "lowly", "heaven" – but she is firmly on the mystical or occult wing (much conventional Christianity regarding the fallen material world as, at the least, unfortunate). In 'Swans', Oliver calls the flying birds "immaculate", and feels their "shoulder-power / echoing / inside my own body". She adores them, and yet they are as "unreachable" as Keats's nightingale: love as belief, not possession.

She does, in a poem about an absent male humming-bird, admit that her "commitment" to "another world" carries an "if": that other world may not exist. All but comically, in a long poem on sensing the "holiness" of river, stone and moss, she confesses, "I don't know who God is exactly". Faith, however, has an "incomparably lovely / young-man voice" and carries his sandals as he walks off, singing. Oliver rejects, as Emerson did, prayer's more selfish ends; these poems (at times indistinguishable from prayer) look outward to the "enchanted" adventure of life, full of "hope". There are no clever or breathtaking lines in this collection, few scintillating figures of speech and the imagery is entirely traditional. But the voice is authentic, as fresh as a painting by an Early American primitive. Even the poem 'Halleluiah' somehow won me over, finishing:

> Halleluiah, I'm sixty now, and even a little more,
> and some days I feel I have wings.

The Scottish poet John Glenday's is a quieter voice, modest to the edge of silence. This silence is the absence of God, which is also a "shadow". There is love, however, which in these poems appears as both an individual thing and a governing creative principle, it having "shaped that absent wind against a tree" (a complex thought, but ballad-like). The prevalence of the spiritual realm recalls John Burnside's work, and Glenday is similarly unafraid of a lexical field that can include "heart's breath", "moment's light" and "lingering soul", although he is equally happy to turn to urban detritus ("drifts of knotted condoms") when required.

Remarkably good at evoking the "hungry, old, surrounding sea", its "pluck and lift", Glenday appears happiest on the wild edge of things, "where Scotland at long last / wearies of muttering its own name", as he puts it in 'A Westray Prayer'. In such places it is easier to reconcile infinity with an absence of answers, or the ocean's mindlessness with faith – as in the superb 'Mangurstadh', where the first stanza seethes through to the end, saving it from banality:

> I send you the hush and founder
> of the waves at Mangurstadh
>
> in case there is too much
> darkness in you now
>
> and you need to remember
> why it is we love

Dorothy Molloy died of cancer ten days before the publication by Faber of her first collection, *Hare Soup*: this third volume consists of leavings collated by her husband. Unsurprisingly, death haunts what is otherwise a jaunty voice, guilelessly unafraid of offering us "mountainy cows", "oh prithee" and a bag that "humdy-dumdies / down the stairs". Time is running out – "I used to be yearning / but now I've no time for such things" – yet "It's a scream" rather than a tragedy. Still, tragedy it was. Starting late following a career as a painter, Molloy was a natural: her work is courageous fun with a dash of darkness. There are awkwardnesses here, doubtless to do with the poems' recovered state: I'm not sure "the rubies he slung round her neck. What the heck" would have survived her blue pen. Most noticeable is an emphasis on fledglings, as if dying is (as Mary Oliver also suggests), "the first stretch of the wings". The final effect is sunny, even when the poet imagines, in Michael Longley mode, her own funeral – as a copy of Emily Dickinson's.

Mary Oliver regards the consuming by a buzzard of a miscarried lamb as a "ceremony" that nature gives thanks for: Fiona Benson, in the first of

Faber's pamphlet series for new poets, likens a similar scene to her own miscarriage, at the grisly end of which "I got up, / gathered my bedding / and walked." This Biblical nod gives the key note of her work: a flower likened to "Christ's sacred heart", the "stoup" of her womb, a "halo" of flowers on a cactus – belief as apparatus, explicit rather than implicit, uncomfortably mingling with the word "fuck" (twice). While the verse is at times promising (a dead bird's claws "pushed out as if skidding to a halt"), Benson has not yet wrestled free of her impressive list of poetry teachers. She needs, perhaps, a dose of Oliver's loose-limbed primitivism along with Molloy's sense of fun.

Adam Thorpe's sixth collection, *From The Neanderthal*, is forthcoming in July from Cape.

Water, Water Everywhere

SARAH WARDLE

Imtiaz Dharker, *Leaving Fingerprints*, Bloodaxe, £8.95, ISBN 9781852248499;
Philip Gross, *The Water Table*, Bloodaxe, £8.95, ISBN 9781852248529;
Alice Kavounas, *Ornament of Asia*, Shearsman, £8.95, ISBN 9781848610613;
Grace Nichols, *Picasso, I Want My Face Back*, Bloodaxe,
£7.95, ISBN 9781852248505;
Caroline Bird, *Watering Can*, Carcanet, £9.95, ISBN 9781847770882.

Like all her books, Imtiaz Dharker's fourth collection, *Leaving Fingerprints*, is illustrated by her soulful drawings and the poems themselves are deep and generous, touching as the traces of her motifs. The book's preface is a quote from her father's copy of Faiz that she packed when she ran away from home: "Give some tree the gift of green again. / Let one bird sing." This timely motto for both East and West is the theme on which all the poems and illustrations are variations, from the image of a woman mending the jigsaw of the universe to an inner song of feminine spirit. When an executioner's handiwork bricks up a young woman who has offended an emperor, her singing, like the "one bird" is heard, as if "a letter from Berlin [...] a song from Belfast, a poem from Dublin".

The poems move from Mumbai to Britain, from universe to self. Fingerprints are variously a lover's touch, a handed-down recipe, a battlefield's footprints, a mental road map, language, speech and palm-readers' predictions, mirroring the thumb-like swirls the poet sees in earth, trees and sky. Clues and traces fill the book, but so do alibis: "Unfixed at last I become the tumbling stream." The word-choice is predominantly natural, legendary and abstract, evoking a comforting and ubiquitous permanence.

In his eighth collection, *The Water Table*, Philip Gross also meditates on permanence in a world of flux, using the Severn Sea as a theme to explore the shifts of human life and murky conundrums. The 'Betweenland' sequence wends through the book, taking the reader on a journey through mid-life. The opening poem makes clear this is personal poetry, where "our world, small craft" can "come through"; but by the closing poem we are left in no doubt that these lyrics have universal relevance in a world of confluence, where "the river was flowing, the flowing was still" and one can no longer discern "which was the father, which was the son", where "the sea was the river, the river the sea". In a very British poem the sea, which had gone on strike, sees invaders crossing and, like a benign Poseidon, "gave an audible sigh and came back in". Elsewhere, an excavated cup holds the hint of the dead on its lip and a river mouth "spoke the hills' / native language in the lowlands' slow / translation". Gross has a gift for fluency and sparkling clarity. His poems hold together like atoms in water, colliding with one another long after you have finished the book.

Alice Kavounas's third book, *Ornament of Asia*, reads like a first collection, so full is it of childhood, family, memory, all the elements that form a poet's identity. These are lyrical poems of her own belonging and the previous generation's displacement. The collection opens paying homage to Homer and Cavafy, but Ithaca turns out to be Cornell, the road to it an icy highway and her father "no Greek / hero, just a man trying to hold his own / in America". Her poems range from New York to the contested landscape of Ionia. In 'Peter Pan Diner' she records outgrowing her roots against the refrain of a juke box song. The title poem pictures the 1922 fall of Smyrna, as of Troy, with "orphans of the 20th century: / Armenians... Jews... Ottoman Greeks... Palestinians... / exiled on the wrong side of history". Her poems have depth and breadth. A sequence, 'The Red Sofa' is threaded through the book, interweaving childhood memories with the wider history of the collection. The sequence is in poetic prose, repeating "mother" and "piano" like echoes, while 'Lure' exhibits her artist's eye for detail: she paints poems you can step into.

Grace Nichols' sixth collection, *Picasso, I Want My Face Back*, has four parts, opening with the title poem, a monologue in the voice of Picasso's sitter and mistress, Dora Maar, the 'Weeping Woman'. Through the sequence Maar progresses from "a clown and a broken / piece of crockery" to a stronger character who can say, "Now I see I was more an accomplice / to my own unrooting". Nichols makes whole again the disjointed sitter, though she warns that there will always be a weeping woman, crying a "Hiroshima of tears". The second part, 'Framing the Landscape', takes as its subject the art, landscape and memory of Guyana and England. We hear music in the language. 'Test Match High Mass' pictures Jesus playing cricket, "Watching his white-clad disciples / work the green fields – tracking the errant red soul / of a ball". The third part, 'Eclipse', looks at world moments, a peace march, Baghdad, New York and Delhi, giving a voice to the Empire State Building, Ophelia and the Lady of the Taj.

Nichols is a master of persona and has an ear for character and tone. The book's final part conjures the character, 'Laughing Woman', written this time in the third person: "Where Mona choose – smile / she choose – laugh". 'The Big Giggle' is a tour de force, setting out Laughing Woman's theory of the universe with "Helium / upsetting the equation", not the Big Bang but "the giggle-effect". Nichols writes in language as dancing and vibrant as Picasso's shapes and colours.

In her third book, *Watering Can*, Caroline Bird, a poet still in her mid-twenties, writes of friends who have given birth and of funerals, looks back at her own past and out at the future. She effortlessly sustains a conceit, as in 'Seesaw', which describes her friend's increasing responsibilities: "one of us grows, the other shrinks". 'The Golden Kids' reads like a class register of obituaries and has a poised tone and maturity from one so young. 'Poet in the Class' echoes Carol Ann Duffy, though doesn't quite measure up. 'Stage Kiss' is a fine poem on the gap between romance and reality with mirrors within mirrors. 'Expecting Rain' watches a funeral with an anthropologist's eye, before the observer steps back into the frame and finds love after life's storms. 'University Poetry Society' is satire which flies. Meanwhile, 'Impartial Information' is a life-affirming list of council services, with a punch-line exhorting a depressive to think twice: it should be available on prescription. Bird says of her own work that her poems are "all the fertiliser that pours on top of your head". With *Watering Can* her imagination is in bloom.

Sarah Wardle's latest collection is *A Knowable World* (Bloodaxe, 2009).

This review was written before the T.S.Eliot prize-winner was announced.

On The Move

SARAH CROWN

Peter Riley, *Greek Passages*, Shearsman Books, £9.95, ISBN 978-1848610514;
Richard Price, *Rays*, Carcanet, £9.95, ISBN 9781847770103;
Alice Notley, *Above the Leaders*, Veer Books, £4, ISBN 9780955876318;
Peter Abbs, *Voyaging Out*, Salt, £12.99, ISBN 9781844715121;
Luke Kennard, *The Migraine Hotel*, Salt, £8.99, ISBN 978-1844715558

Travel of one kind or another drives the action in each of these collections, most clearly in the first of our five, Peter Riley's *Greek Passages*. Through his book (the title of which enfolds a double meaning, grammatical and geographical) Riley takes the reader on a tour of Greece, a land of holidays and history, via a series of prose-poems, each set out on its own page like a diary entry, or postcard home.

There's a faint but unmistakable tang of the travel brochure here, strongest in Riley's sweetly simple, opening observations of scenes which, though elegantly rendered (a stretch of coastline composed of "treatises of light, waves of soft rock"; an evening at a bar where "Slim as pencils the leaves / throw themselves at the music"), are a touch misty-eyed. Happily, during the central sections, written during extended trips to Argos, the poems richen. The "passages" of the title are no longer mere tourist trips: the poet drills down into the past, unearthing not only "Phoenician traders" and "Helen of the war", but his personal history of "dark northern towns, complex of small back streets I can't quite remember". The two histories intertwine with fragments of song and poetry and the air and sea of modern-day Greece to produce what Riley, in a lovely late hymn to the people ("peasants, builders, workers, suppliers, teachers") "of whom nothing remains", calls "movements of grace on the offered instant".

Peter Abbs's *Voyaging Out* is split into two sections: 'Peregrinations' and 'Transformations'. The second comprises deft reworkings of poems from Rumi, Dante and Rilke, but is far outshone by the first, in Abbs' own voice, in which he journeys outward through the world and inward through the treasury of his head, in poems that take on everything from Philip Larkin (pictured fondly "holding cycle-clips in the cool aisles / of the lost churches of lost England") to language itself.

It is place, however, that lies at the heart of this collection. Abbs grew up in Norfolk, and its spaciousness is evident in poems whose landscapes are soft-rimmed, borders flexible, and whose ever-present birds ("oyster catchers [...] flying out across the sands, / wings to wing in unison", a swan powering overhead, "webbed feet dripping silver // in the mist") are dream-like, half-lit. Snow is a constant presence, too, "ghosting the trees, cowling the sun", muting edges and diffusing light. In 'Love's Landscapes', perhaps the finest moment in a fine collection, he combines all that's best of his work, joining philosophical reflections on what, precisely, the nature of such "landscapes" might be with ventures into memory and vital representations of the here-and-now: "the winter room" where "in the grate the wood blazes against the burning rings / of soot". "Here time suspends its reckless flight", the speaker says, and that's what we take from this collection: a breathing space, tranquilised and rhapsodic, from which to consider the world.

Alice Notley's journeys are those of the *flaneur*. Her poems criss-cross the *arondissements* of Paris, telling the city's stories; her wilder flights – of language and imagination – anchored by street names and shop fronts. Images of place and people bump up against one another, overlapping to form a "city of texture of a chestnut", crammed to overflowing with *boulangeries*, metro stations, meetings, misfortunes and the constant threat and promise of sex. Notley's attempts to realise the city are echoed in her efforts to conjure herself. It's a plainly Whitmanesque venture, and his shadow hangs over her poems; she references him directly ("You're only thinking of yourself / not the reading or Whitman," she challenges a speaker) and indirectly, in her acts of creation ("Rivers I sang, mountains I began") and self-definition ("I am my luck, my figure, my history, my fire, / and my house"). At worst, her homages can be confusing and unwieldy, her lines overstuffed and unmediated; at best, however, they meld with an expat's crisp perception of the city to create poems that are dense, populous pleasures.

In our final pair, the journeying moves from the physical into the formal. Richard Price and Luke Kennard appear to have set themselves the task of investigating poetry itself, testing its boundaries, pressing up against its limits. While both go about this with a playfulness that makes each collection a pleasure to read, their approaches differ.

Love is the subject of Price's third collection, *Rays*. He opens with an antic sizzle: a reworking of Sonnet XVIII in which he manages the scarcely credible feat of taking on the Bard and holding his own, coming up with a closing couplet ("So long as folk can breathe or eyes can see / so this will live, and this gives life to you and me") that actually expands on the original. After this, however, the bulk of the poems are distillations; seekings-out of the essence of the words that we use to describe love. Insomnia is a recurring motif, and there is a flavour here of those moments on the edge of consciousness where words fall into each other and sense is derived as much from sound and rhythm as it is from meaning. In the beautiful 'Langour's Whispers', words slide and elide to create the lush eroticism of lines such as "Touch, and touch's could-be / deep shallows, lap / and kiss, sense-sipping lips, / finger-tips." In Price's poetry, as in love, language hovers on the brink of dissolution.

In *The Migraine Hotel* (which traces a direct line from 2007's heady *The Harbour Beyond the Movie*), on the other hand, Kennard gives himself room. Poems unspool over pages as he seeks to find space for idiosyncratic forays into territory that includes film criticism, *schadenfreude* ("My friend, your irresponsibility and your unhappiness delight me. Your financial problems and your expanding waist-line are a constant source of relief"), shopping centres and, *via* the welcome return of Wolf – surely one of the finest serio-comic creations to spring into being anywhere in literature in recent years – the questionable benefits of psychoanalysis and the thorny issue of national identity. If these cantankerous comic monologues locate him in the Baudelarian tradition, however, there's nothing anachronistic about this collection; Kennard's sensibility is firmly twenty-first century. One of the funniest moments in a regularly laugh-out-loud collection comes in 'The Six Times My Heart Broke'. "The third time my heart broke," says the speaker,

> I had my heart removed and replaced by a donor heart. I dipped my former heart into a container of liquid nitrogen and dropped in onto a paving slab where it smashed. 'Art project', I explained to a pedestrian.

Thank heaven for Luke Kennard. As thought-provoking and poignant as it's witty, this collection confirms him as an exceptional – in every sense – voice in poetry today.

Sarah Crown is the Editor of Guardian Online.

The Knack

ALAN BROWNJOHN

Herbert Lomas, *A Casual Knack of Living: Collected Poems*,
Arc, £14.99, ISBN 9781906570521

T he title of Herbert Lomas's large, exuberant – and overdue – *Collected Poems*, a four hundred-page volume easy to browse and enjoy but hard to summarise, comes from an unremembered, yet once re-read unforgettable, early poem by Alan Ross, 'Survivors'. Rescued from an icy sea "with the ship burning in their eyes", the sailors on an Arctic mission taking supplies to a Soviet Union landlocked by war later recall "the confusion and the oily dead", and sense how casual the "knack" (an inspired word) of normal, moment-to-moment living actuality is.

More later about the appropriateness of Lomas's title to the contents of his book. It's interesting to note first that in a brief preface (called simply 'A Word') he emphasises that his sixty-year output may be lightened by humour but essentially reflects

> an incredibly cruel and mismanaged world, and the horrors and
> the mismanagement are still going on

He wants his poems to present a "developing" observer of his age, not only the wider horrors he can do little about but his profound personal loss and sadness. We soon see that they will not be a record of, or commentary on, events, but a series of strategies he has somehow acquired for coping with them – through a knack of understanding?

Born in 1924, Lomas saw army service on the north-west frontier ("the boredoms and humiliations of soldiering" subsequently recorded in *A Useless Passion* (1998)), went to Liverpool University, taught in London and Helsinki (receiving a notable honour for translating, and spreading the word about, Finnish literature), became an attentive and charitable critic for Alan Ross's *London Magazine* and *Ambit*, penned a short polemic on money-worship; and constantly produced poems! The earliest to reach a general readership were six with a distinct sixties pop poetry flavour in Michael Horovitz's Penguin "Underground" anthology *Children of Albion* in 1969, the same year as his first book, *Chimpanzees are Blameless Creatures*, was published. Only one is preserved here; Lomas was no follower of fashion and already more interested in asking questions and pursuing ideas, sometimes prophetically: "Can we make buying and selling money / the main business till the big bang / reverses and contracts / towards the crunch?"

In the mid-Seventies and Eighties the poems become more meditative, more rueful, although several spirited versions of Horace odes suggest the benefits accruing from translation work. This is a sensual poetry, full of, yes, a casual delight in living, but sometimes occasionally trapped in worried argument, as in *Hamlet*: "What we really want to do / Is write, find / Verbal solutions for the universe". One important influence is gratefully acknowledged in one of his very best poems, 'Auden at his Villa on Ischia', in *Public Footpath* (1981). But Lomas charts a less relaxed progress into his Christian faith than the master, and it is not only readers who don't share it who find the variable fifty-two sections of the Dantesque *Letters in the Dark* (1986) a harder proposition: a modern man groping for security in religion without the infrastructure of certainties in a Herbert or Hopkins.

With his adjournment to life in Aldeburgh in his Sixties he finds not only a focus for some of his most approachable – and finest – later work, but time to explore and expand the memories of childhood and early manhood that lurked as small, poignant or sinister, reference in the early books: *The Vale of Todmorden* (part 1981 and part 2003; thus a remarkable achievement of his late seventies) finely recreates, in commanding detail, both a personal world and one familiar to his forebears; as in 'Depression': "malignant spirits materialise at will [...] / they hang about outside my bedroom door [...] / I feel safer in clothes. // I get in bed with them on. In the photo my face is pale, overtired, / with dark rings round the eyes, / knowing the black-winged bat behind me // filling the pavements with the unemployed." The world remains "mismanaged", but readers of this rich and formidable *Collected* will feel rewarded by the strategies – the "clothes"? – Herbert Lomas offers for surviving in it.

Alan Brownjohn's *Ludbrooke, And Others* is forthcoming from Enitharmon in the summer.

Living Poetry

ALISON BRACKENBURY

Jon Glover, *Magnetic Resonance Imaging*, Carcanet,
£9.95, ISBN 9781857549676;
E.A.Markham, *Looking Out, Looking in*, Anvil, £14.95, ISBN 9780856464140;
Robert Conquest, *Penultimata*, Waywiser, £8.99, ISBN 9781904130369;
Larissa Miller, *Guests of Eternity*, Arc, £12.99, ISBN 9781904614883

Should poets' biographies touch our reading of their poetry? In theory, perhaps not. But no single theory explains the workings of a poem. In the case of these four poets, I think it is helpful to let life – briefly – brush against literature.

Jon Glover, in a postscript, refers to his "experiences of being diagnosed with MS", and to his aim for his poems: "seeing (seeing as?) knowable and un-knowable worlds". This does illuminate the strikingly unusual workings of his poems. 'Coal Bags' begins with fiercely physical description:

> coarse, tarry
> fibre between sharp, black rock and a man's
> back; a muscular, shining energy

but ends with a single, startling word: "syllables". The buried power of coal has been compressed into a vision of the power of words, "seeing as". Glover's poems see into what is normally un-knowable, "infinitely splitting particles". The poems themselves, like a centrifuge, spin out different elements, sometimes in sonnet or ballad, but most typically in quicksilver lines unweighed by rhyme. Fragmentary phrases with nouns –"Between the stone steps" – are followed by endearingly dramatic interjections, like "Boo" ('Snakes Again'). Occasionally, I was frustrated by a lack of narrative. But Glover's lines often intrigue, glancing into beauty, "listening, as ghosts, transparent / with their imagined perfect hiss."

As the book progresses, the poems' disparate elements begin to settle into more knowable endings, sometimes desperate, sometimes resigned: "there's no help, no earthly help" ('More Trash') "Everything has to go" ('Site'). I was particularly moved by the book's final section, with its simple lists of trades and names:

Martha and Lilly Glover.

Lilly was 8 and Martha 14. She worked

with table knives.   ('Burnishing')

It is no accident that the final poem of Glover's courageous and lovely tilt at intractable facts ends with the word "praised".

Looking Out, Looking in, selected work by E.A. Markham, begins boldly with a substantial section of first-class new poems. Their energy leaps off the page. "'Generous!' shrieks the husband." The selection from eight previous collections reveals barer early poems, jabbing at stereotypes: "I am not a mugger, madam." But Markham's strengths are remarkably constant. "World traveller, me", he remarks genially in a late poem (set on a Sheffield train), and all these poems open onto a world far beyond Sheffield: in Africa, where a child has "a burnt-out bus for home", or the aftermath of revolution, where, as Markham observes sardonically, it is "Safe now to write a little poem".

The violence of life, domestic and political, stalks Markham's poems. A mother beats her son, "she bathing him with licks". A kitten, in a nightmare nursery rhyme, is killed in a yard "Where the dogs still lie in wait". This work waylays its readers with a whole armoury of final twists: "the light blows out. / I'm sitting in the dark; there are Christians about". Even his place names keep readers on their toes. Markham was born in Montserrat, but you will not find his poems' island, St. Caesare, on the map. Yet "memory / is your hinterland", as Markham writes to Derek Walcott, and a Caribbean grandmother presides over poem after poem "like a god". A late poem mourns "the riches of home", "the cassava smell has gone". In a prose epilogue, Markham writes "the music of words, when strung together [...] hints at those elusive joys of living".

Markham died in 2008, but his "strung together" lines still play upon the reader: crackling with life.

The elegance and liveliness of Robert Conquest's poetry skim depths suggested by his lovely quotation from De Musset, "*si triste et profonde*". The poems flow in cadences which draw an intricate net of echoes and names into their wake:

> Light, lighter than snow
> Falls on the Savernake
> And streams down the upper Stour
>
> As she too leans from a window [...]

Conquest has an equally fine ear for speech. "'Perfect's a word you mustn't use', / She said". The poems in *Penultimata* depend upon perfect poise, and only occasionally slip from their tightrope. The balance of the tender and acerbic is held beautifully during 'In Attendance'. Conquest observes lovers, surrounded by "lice-ridden" pigeons, but concludes "Let's call them doves". 'The Last Day (Embarkation Leave)' ends with a mirror image of a couple's ecstasy: "To merge again? Not certainly. Not soon". An unsparing historian of the Soviet system, Conquest notes in 'The Idea of Virginia' that the American ideal was "never fulfilled", but "never abandoned".

These vigorous poems have an exquisite colour sense: St Petersburg's light is "ermine, almond". They linger wittily over longing: "There'll be no naiads in that rill / So let's forget about them. (Still…)" They are irreverent to the cosmos, "Sod of a sun!" and, with a nod to Larkin, savage to biographers: "They fuck you up". Robert Conquest was born in 1917 and the lightness and sharpness of this writing remain exemplary to all of us who are under ninety. With its long-drawn out falls and quickfire wit, it is a restorative music.

Sasha Dugdale mourns in her introduction that Larissa Miller's poems possess "a musicality […] hard to reproduce in English". But Richard McKane's clear, eloquent translations reveal poetry of extraordinary power. Even the briefest phrase can be radiant with the possibilities of "the unbounded earth". "Every moment is a mystery". It is humbling to learn that Miller had a harsh post-war childhood in Soviet Russia, where her dissident husband was later imprisoned. These poems, written during four decades, were not published until the 1990s, in a collection called *Between the Cloud and the Pit*. Miller's short intense lyrics encompass both:

> When they led away the innocent under guard
> the cherry trees were blossoming tenderly […]
> in those black, black years.

The poet's extraordinary range is shown in her poems about her son, from the apocalyptic "the cradle is hanging over an abyss" to the ruefully affectionate "your mother, tiresome and tender". Some poems declare themselves starkly: "How can you measure / truth, good and evil?" Others try, like winter's "snow-white threads", to link "the unearthly and the earthly". Her work is both sensuous and passionately religious. One poem calls "Come here" to a lover; another cries "O Lord". Yet Miller is unaffectedly human, relishing tea and "honey cake". Her work is rich in reference to rhythm, "breaths in and out", and the "yearning" for rhyme. The parallel text reveals how often the ecstatic rush of her poems depends, throughout the decades, on intricate rhymes; and she has written how hard it is "to maintain order in that space [...] our souls". Yet music orders the space of her poems. The power of Larissa Miller's work restores ones faith not simply in poetry, but in life itself.

Alison Brackenbury's essay on the influence of John Clare appears on pp.70-75.

Rebounding Flowerheads

DAVID MORLEY

The Hundred Thousand Places, Thomas A. Clark, Carcanet,
£9.95, ISBN 9781847770059;
Lines of Sight, Frances Presley, Shearsman Books,
£12.99, ISBN 9781848610392;
Hangman's Acre, Janet Sutherland, Shearsman Books,
£9.95, ISBN 9781848610743;
The Sun Fish, Eiléan Ní Chuilleanáin, Gallery Books,
€11.95, ISBN 9781852354824

For Thomas A. Clark, walking is a form of poetry, a personal rite for writing. *The Hundred Thousand Places* is a single poem that steps through the Scottish wilds over the space of a day. It moves forward through subtle quatrains, the pauses between them invisibilized by a blank page: a cloud coming across the vision. And inner and outer vision are really what this poet offers in gently-sculpted, clear-eyed variations:

> the rock in the water
> breaking the full
> weight of the flow
> produces melody

the rock by the water
broken by bracken
tormentil and heather
releases colour

    Solvitur ambulando – it is solved by walking; and the world is a series of connected and out of the ordinary problems that might be solved only by moving through them. As Rebecca Solnit wrote in *Wanderlust: A History of Walking*, "Walking shares with making and working that crucial element of engagement of the body and the mind with the world, of knowing the world through the body and the body through the world". For Thomas A. Clark, walking doesn't solve anything in any final way; it explores and perhaps resolves in part the problem of our ultimate loneliness. The short poems that make up the whole poem possess a strict sense of precision inherited from Ian Hamilton Finlay: a summation of perception and connection which could be carved on a granite slab in Little Sparta:

from rock
heather
from astringency
colour

I'm sure Clark would agree with Solnit's statement that "A lone walker is both present and detached, more than an audience but less than a participant. Walking assuages or legitimizes this alienation." Thomas A. Clark's lovely and somewhat lonely poem releases many valuable visions and a deep sense for the music of the natural world. I also think the poetry explores a form of legitimized alienation, something more than an audience and less than a participant; and is more honest to itself and its readers for doing so.

    Like Thomas A. Clark's book, Frances Presley's *Lines of Sight* takes many a wild walk through the natural landscape, this time in the South West of England. *Lines of Sight* also reads as though it were written as a whole book, so scrupulously have the sections and poems been woven and riven together. Richly impressive are the poems from 'Stones settings and longstones', a highly kynaesthetic sequence inspired by the Neolithic stone monuments on Exmoor. Prose poems, concrete poems and free verse are madly and delightfully mixed with arresting artistic control and design, which makes them almost slippery when quoted out of context:

               Not against wind
               we have won wind

               the house is standing against
               abutting the hillside
                              abetting

               buttery butts
               the water but
               cannot save australia

                    this sliver of stone

               compressed
               glivers
               revested   ('Buttery stone')

     The prehistoric stone monuments on Exmoor are evocative and strange:
geometric arrangements of sandstone slabs in quiet combes; willowy standing
stones on open moors; and stone rows, one of which was only recently
discovered. The geometric and highly patterned orchestration of Presley's
book echoes these forms. I found her work a highly pleasant revelation, at
once thoroughly alert and judged yet delightfully manic and far-reaching in
its wildness, risks and resultant freedoms.
     Janet Sutherland prefers a pared-back, uncluttered, free verse for the
poems in *Hangman's Acre*. The understated tones and hewn forms create a
careful performance (there's a call to be made for poems, like these, whose
proximity to pain and death is pretty well face to face). But Sutherland's
poems do not gloom or mope; and like the poets above she is a gifted and
observant nature writer:

               the voice of the chainsaw echoes in
               valleys   smoke hangs high and drifts
               the terraces are held against the mountain
               by the dead and the living   their hands

               their muscles   the salt of their skin
               at dusk the mountains shift to grey
               layers of rock are smoke and mist
               and the sound of the chainsaw stops

> just this spade and this pick scraping
> making the little difference   and underfoot
> the cloudy cyclamen and by the side
> the dark-leaved aromatic myrtle   ('Underfoot')

There are many delicacies in such an approach: deftness of image, delays of space. Elizabeth Bishop's attentiveness of voice hangs over this whole collection but the influence is one of tone. I can't help but admire the fact this poet can yield such music, movement and scent from a rebounding flowerhead and a slowed-down spondee-sprung myrtle.

Eiléan Ní Chuilleanáin's *Selected* was recently co-published by Gallery and Faber. *The Sun Fish* is to my mind her best single volume. It contains an impressive number of outstanding poems, including 'The Witch in the Wardrobe', 'On Lacking the Killer Instinct', 'The Door', 'Ascribed', 'Calendar Custom' and the title poem. Any reader new to this poet would do well to begin with these poems and to read them out loud, taking aural delight in the rhyme-patterns and stanza break in 'The Door' for example, quoted here in whole:

> When the door opened the lively conversation
> Beyond it paused very briefly and then pushed on;
> There were sounds of departure, a railway station,
> Everyone talking with such hurried animation
> The voices could hardly be told apart until one
>
> Rang in a sudden silence: 'The word when, that's where you start –'
> Then they all shouted goodbye, the trains began to tug and slide;
> Joyfully they called while the railways pulled them apart
> And the door discreetly closed and turned from a celestial arch
> Into merely a door, leaving us cold on the outside.

Read alongside her *Selected Poems*, *The Sun Fish* makes a profoundly convincing case for Eiléan Ní Chuilleanáin's international reputation. The former volume reached the T.S. Eliot Prize shortlist, and I hope this makes her work deservedly better known in the United Kingdom.

David Morley's next collection from Carcanet is *Enchantment* (2010). He is co-editing *The Cambridge Companion to Creative Writing*. www.davidmorley.org.uk

At Home In The World

ANDRÉ NAFFIS-SAHELY

Yang Lian, *Lee Valley Poems*, Bloodaxe, £9.95, ISBN

"London? It's one of the countless foreign towns I've drifted through," Yang Lian informs us in his preface to *Lee Valley Poems*, his latest volume. Years earlier, in *Ghost Talk*, written in Auckland in the early nineties, Lian had likened "home'" to an old house with a leaking roof. "Every day as you climb the stairs you think: 'so this is exile'. You could write each flight as a chapter, the two-story house could be written as a great historical epic on the exile of mankind. But it still wouldn't be you. You cannot speak of these elusive feelings, so whenever someone mentions reality, all you ever want to do is laugh." If not much humour, there is much *joie de vivre* in *Lee Valley Poems*, a lot of it in the wry reflections that pepper the book – as in 'Home':

> A poet needs a cave   no smaller than
> his intolerable stupidity,   the walls change and change again
> and a painting hung on the emptiness   makes itself at
>   home in the wind.

By changing the valley's spelling from 'Lea' to 'Lee', Lian writes himself into his adopted geography – 'Lee' is a Chinese surname – and why not? It has taken him sixteen years, but it finally seems as if the "ghost" has forged a link between his language and surroundings, and, as Lian affirms in the preface, made London his local – his first local since his post-Tienanmen exile. At first glance, *Lee Valley Poems* seems a more approachable offering than his previous effort, a philosophical epic entitled *Concentric Circles*. *Lee Valley Poems*, however, is ambitious in scope. It is divided into two halves – *Section One: Shorter Poems*, a collection of lyrics and elegies – and *Section Two: A Sequence, What Water Confirms*, where Lian takes us from Leipzig to the banks of the Hudson – and all the way back to the hustle of Hackney – swept along on the "interstellar   loneliness of water."

A few words on the translation itself. Whereas Lian's previous volumes were handled exclusively by Brian Holton and Agnes Hung-Chong Chan, *Lee Valley Poems* adopts a more complex approach. Thanks to Pascale Petit,

Fiona Sampson, Polly Clark, Jacob Edmond, W.N. Herbert, Antony Dunn and Arthur Sze, Lian's poems come to us in a welcome variety of nuances, cadences and rhythms. Translating is a difficult, often thankless task. Lian himself is sympathetic: "you take off borrowed flesh and blood" he writes in 'Brian Holton Travelling in New Zealand', "go where no one is to get good and drunk." The ways these poets succeed makes one wonder why this should be the exception rather than the rule. A translator should be like a passport a poet uses when coming into a foreign country. Leafing through *Lee Valley Poems* is akin to standing in a high security vault while salivating over a safe box full of visas and hard currencies. You feel as if you could go anywhere.

André Naffis-Sahely edits the Poeboes podcast series for Words without Borders.

A Profligacy Of Pamphlets

JACQUELINE GABBITAS

Poems, Noshi Gillani, translated by Lavinia Greenlaw and Nukbah Langah, ISBN 9781904634751; *Poems*, Coral Bracho, translated by Katherine Pierpoint and Tom Boll, ISBN 9781904634782; *Poems*, Toeti Heraty, translated by Carole Satyamurti and Ulrich Kratz, ISBN 9781904634799; *Poems*, Gagan Gill, translated by Jane Duran and Lucy Rosenstein, ISBN 9781904634805; *Poems*, Maxamed Xaashi Dhamac 'Gaarriye, translated by W.N. Herbert and Martin Orwin, ISBN 9781904634737; *Poems*, Farzaneh Khojandi, translated by Jo Shapcott and Narguess Farzad, ISBN 9781904634744; *Poems*, Partaw Naderi, translated by Sarah Maguire and Yama Yari, ISBN 9781904634812; *Poems*, Kajal Ahmad, translated by Mimi Khalvati and Choman Hardi, ISBN 9781904634720; *Poems*, Corsino Fortes, translated by Sean O'Brien and Daniel Hahn, ISBN 9781904634768; *Poems*, Al-Saddiq Al-Raddi, translated by Sarah Maguire and Sabry Hafez, ISBN 9781904634775; ALL POETRY TRANSLATION CENTRE & ENITHARMON PRESS, £4; *Faber New Poets 3*, Heather Phillipson, ISBN 9780571249978; *Faber New Poets 4*, Jack Underwood, ISBN 9780571249985: BOTH FABER & FABER, £5; *Four Elegies*, Paul Driver, New Victoria Press, ISBN 9780956350800; *Singer*, Sally Goldsmith, Smith/Doorstop Books, £4, ISBN 9781906613068;

Party Piece, Anna Woodford, Smith/Doorstop Books, £4, ISBN 9781906613075;
Elegies for the Dead in Cyrenaica, Hamish Henderson,
Polygon, £9.99, ISBN 9781846970931;
The Terrors, Tom Chivers, Nine Arches Press, £5, ISBN 9780956055927;
Emblems, Wayne Burrows, ISBN 9781904886945; *The Shell Hymn Book*, John
Fuller, ISBN: 9781904886952: BOTH SHOESTRING PRESS, £5;
MMV, Andrew O'Donnell, Open Season Press.

The Poetry Translation Centre and Enitharmon Press published ten dual-language chapbooks to introduce the international poets who took part in the PTC's 'World Poets' Tours to a wider English-speaking audience. Many of the poems in the series deal with loss or compromise of language (both written and oral), voice or identity, as in Ahmed's 'Birds' and Gillani's 'This Prisoner Breathes'. Some, like Fortes in 'Emigrant', explore gaining new language and identity; a good number look to recognize or strengthen their place in the world, (lived-in and/or literary) and its responses to them, as in Al-Saddiq's 'Theatre' or Naderi's 'Relative', and strong socio-political themes run throughout the series.

At first I wondered why these were not published as a single anthology. Part of the answer can be found in the decision to publish in dual-languages. These chapbooks are designed to be read on their own as well as part of the series. They are introductions to new poets for English-speaking readers, but also collections by well-established poets with a strong readership in their communities across the UK. Read together they act like an *extended* anthology, but one for which readers create their own order or rationale; this is refreshing in that they are subject to little editorial intervention. One day the poems of Fortes might be followed by those of Gaarriye, the next day by Khojandi. In this rearrangement new things might come out of the work: newly seen alliances, associations or contradictions; freshly heard music – as if parts of the world were talking to one another and each day the conversation is different.

Elsewhere, *MMV* by Andrew O'Donnell is a long political poem taking as its starting point British society after the London bombings in 2005. This book is beautifully produced, though the font-size is unnecessarily tiny. At first the poem seems conventionally written in free-verse triplets, but quickly the reader realizes there are intentional gaps in between words, designed to reflect society's disjunct reasoning – the poem's main theme. Sometimes this works, as in "render up no reason. A desperation, ignored, drives", but in the main it doesn't and becomes irritating. Having said this, the poem has passion and charge and reminds me a little of hearing Adrian Mitchell reading his versions of Brecht at Poetry International.

Jack Underwood is one of the Faber New Poets. His are clever poems, many of them mysterious, especially early on in this collection. I liked the ending of 'Migration' for its clean sentiment, "I will try the border again tomorrow. // But not before it's my turn / and I must break the neck of a bird / that has flown here for the winter." Some of the poems are consciously poetic in their language, as in 'How shall I say this?' and some are much freer, more relaxed and convincing because of it: 'Currency' is successful where the reader believes the events because of the language, which is almost reportage; "She touches my left palm / to her right kidneys, asks in a neat foreign whisper, 'I have been waiting / for you?' "What else can I say but 'Yes' and 'For me'?"

The most successful poem in Paul Driver's *Four Elegies* is 'Georgie Broon'. George Mackay Brown was an Orkney poet and playwright and 'Georgie Broon' is a warm and affectionate poem that doesn't hide the difficulties of Brown's life – particularly his shyness and alcoholism – but treats them simply as facts. The end is elegant, playful and attentive to its subject as well as its reader, "and when I asked you at the festival, / would you take a bow tonight, you seemed the mildest man / in corn-patched Orkney / when you said, 'Oh no, I'd die'."

At sixty-three pages, Hamish Henderson's *Elegies for the Dead in Cyrenaica* is more a slim volume than a pamphlet. It is a collection of elegies and a song. The greatest pleasures I found in reading it were in what I learned about this area of Libya, the sense of comradeship between the soldiers of the fighting countries, and the music/language/authenticity of the poems' voices. 'The End of a Campaign' is beautiful in its simple diction and natural syntax and asks a question we might not expect of a soldier-poet, especially in a war in which propaganda was a violent weapon, "There were our own, there were the others. / Their deaths were like their lives, human and animal [...] why should I not sing of them, the dead, the innocent?". The language throughout is fresh and contemporary: these poems could have been written yesterday. Compare "We know that our minds are as slack and rootless / as the tent-pegs driven into cracks of limestone [...]" from 'El Adem', with "The heat in the pavement escapes like steam, / turns storefronts to jelly, melts stone into the air" from Wayne Burrows's 'IV: The Illusion'. Yet these two collections have sixty years between them.

The root of Burrows's *Emblems*, however, goes back much further: it's written after the seventeenth century poet Francis Quarles's *Emblems*. Burrows's emblems are intelligent, unassuming poems with quiet, dark-edged humour. Each poem has an epigraph that works to the poem's benefit; Burrows doesn't try to extend the epigraphs or re-create the original poems, as a lesser poet might, he uses them to find a new poem, a different subject space. 'The Headlines' appealed to me particularly. A poignant mixture of narrative description, newspaper headlines and dialogue, it describes a re-trained carpenter making a table and telling his story of working in the City as the world continues around him, heard through the radio, "the echo of traffic noise", "the sound of tide turning back inland, / waves choppy as stock-market graphs." By the poem's end we are reminded of the carpenter's (and our own) mortality, "He stoops, kneels. / Taps joints locked tight as bones in skulls".

Similarly historical in conceit is *The Terrors*, Tom Chivers's sequence of imagined emails to inmates incarcerated at Newgate Prison, London, in the eighteenth century. The idea is clever and the poems are well researched but don't give too much away as to the identity of their recipients. Overall, the collection is funny and dark: 'Murder by inches' charts the tortures that Elizabeth Browrigg conducted on her servants and ends with the line "You've gone viral, Liz." (Browrigg was arrested when a servant died of infected wounds.)

In *Singer*, Sally Goldsmith is a poet who also loves story-telling, and who flits between the past and the present effortlessly. She plays with narrative familiarities such as fairytales, and creates atmosphere well, as in the intimate space of 'The Singer'. Goldsmith has a keen eye, as seen in "the dead bumble-bee in a cough drop tin", "the pedal car with one pedal and the still spinning top" from 'You'll know her'. I have reservations about some of the lineation; in the sestina, 'Song', some of the line breaks following "gone" draw too much attention to the word, "[…]after everyone has gone / to bed[…]", "[…] daylight is gone / into moon night". […] But when they do work, they work well – "Now the weight of the world is gone – / the walls lift and float.[…]".

Anna Woodford also creates intimate but universal poems in her *Party Piece*. She is good at taking potentially clichéd subject matter and transforming or elevating it, as in 'Feral', "There bodies are unbroken with scant fur and hardened eyes. / They use gravestones like easy chairs." There's nothing cosy about this scene. But I was left unsatisfied, wanting more from the poem because it felt there was more there to give. Here is a poet that loves language – as a toy, a tool, a weapon. In 'Exchange' she delights in its beginnings with the baby who "reports back from on high in a baby-tongue" to a father who "[…]is the Adamest man in the Garden.".

Heather Phillipson, another Faber New Poet, is an intelligent writer with a dry wit, 'Nuts and the Invention of Aspiration' is a good example of this. These poems began to engage me at about page eight, where there was more of an emotional centre to them. Moreover, Phillipson has a habit of taking each off into a different direction at the end whether it's best for it or not, which after a while seems mannered. However, 'Crossing the Col' Aubisque' is a beautiful poem, the ending perfect – it travels distances organically and even tells the reader it's going to do so but without being too self-conscious: "Let me change gear while you drink pear juice. / Beyond your bonnet is the rest of the world. / Mountains – I can barely see them" I'm looking forward to reading the full collection.

I enjoyed *The Shell Hymn Book* by John Fuller partly because they made me question what a hymn is. Those I recalled from my childhood had vibrancy – celebrating their subjects, words and music. And these poems do just that, if at times a little sardonically, as in 'Neither One thing nor the Other'; "A man of sanguine temperament / Came to a barren shore, / And there his sanguine days were spent / Each like the one before." It's easy to conjure up Lear and Carroll with subjects such as crabs, mussels and trumpets, yet these are not poems for children, but barbed with warnings and social-commentary, "Our one illusion is a sport, / That what we gain will somehow last, / Our little empire a mere thought / Of what has passed." ...But then again, aren't all hymns?

Jacqueline Gabbitas's pamphlet is *Mid Lands* (Hearing Eye, 2007). She received a Hawthornden Fellowship in 2009 and edits *Brittle Star*.

ENDPAPERS

from *Cold Eye*, a collaboration between an artist
and a poet to examine the creative process.
(Lintott Press, limited edition, Sept 2010)

Dan Burt and Paul Hodgson
from A Cold Eye

She comes with a train of shadows never cast
By any earthly forms

SIE KOMMT

(…Es ist die Konigen der Nacht…)

Tamino, *The Magic Flute*
Act 1, Scene 2

She comes with a train of shadows never cast
By any earthly forms whose charge and mass
Thwart light; they flutter just beyond my grasp
Like cherry blossoms a puff of wind unclasps.

She comes around the corner of the years
Streaming faux memories from foreign piers
That never were, dreams I would clear
Of unshared passages, landfalls and tears.

She comes and, for a breath, regret recalls
An unmade voyage: our first-born's squall,
Trimming the sheets while teaching her to sail,
Her hand on mine before my father's pall.

Phantoms swimming in my deeps of night,
No magic flute can pipe you to the light.

Letter From Manhattan

JAMES BYRNE

It's near the end of January in Midtown, and morning brings a blizzard. A band of workmen are taking down the skating rink at Bryant Park, which involves collapsing a man-made 'pond' the size of a football field. A bronze Gertrude Stein, squatting Buddha-like and bloated, presides over the repossessed lawn. Although the canopy of plane trees was modelled on the public gardens of Paris, Bryant didn't always conjure up comparisons with the Tuileries. In fact, up until 1980 it was 'dominated by undesirables', a place notorious for drug deals, prostitution and muggings.

The park is fronted by one of New York's most awe-inspiring older buildings, the New York Public Library. I have heard rumours that the NYPL might struggle to survive the credit-crunched Obama administration because of a $23million budget cut. It would be a travesty if this marble *grande dame* were to close. I first visited the library last summer, when they had a small but informative display of photographs marking the fortieth anniversary of the Stonewall riots and the 'birth of the gay rights movement' in the US. Now there's a celebration of two hundred and fifty years since Voltaire's *Candide*. But, today, I am at the beginning of what may become a Calvino-like book-to-book chase. I ignore the exhibitions and head straight to the reading rooms.

Since arriving in New York, I have searched for a poem that might initiate a feeling of honorary citizenship, something essential and beyond the physicality of any given avenue. With so many celebrated resident poets – from Hart Crane to Elizabeth Bishop, Mina Loy to Wallace Stevens – where does my search begin? In my teens, like most kids with a vague interest in New York poetry, I feasted on that unwitting founding father of the 'New York School', Frank O'Hara, replaying stock scenes from his *Lunch* breaks, where he famously went "for a walk among the hum-colored / cabs. First, down the sidewalk where laborers feed their dirty / glistening torsos". But the *mise-en-scène* of O'Hara's *Lunch* poems feels too quick and apprehending, locked into the city's topography. Ditto O'Hara's extraordinary *Second Avenue*, which is delicious as a one-gulper, but not sustaining enough to be kept beside me and read piece-meal through the drawn-out changeability of a year in Manhattan. Last November, my good friend Alfred Corn stopped through New York where I was to record him reading poems for *The Wolf*. In an empty art studio down the hall from the Creative Writing Program at Columbia University (where Alfred once taught) he read from his second collection *A Call in the Midst of the Crowd*, first published in 1975. The title poem threads together a year in New York City, bringing together an auspicious and varied crowd of hardened New Yorkers (like Whitman, Melville, Hart Crane, Poe, Wharton, O'Hara, Henry James and Billie Holiday) whom he enlists for his purposes. There is also a fascinating array of quotes dating right back to Henry Hudson's *Discovery* voyage of 1611. Alfred's *Call* is in four parts and some of the quotes collude with the poems, though the result isn't merely patchwork. His project here is very distinct from, say, the genius of Crane's *White Buildings* or Mayakovsky's 'Brooklyn Bridge'. But all these works rely on time-travel.

Perhaps this continual accounting for one's place is what New York City demands from the poet: participation in the city's history of insatiable literary aspiration. One of Corn's sources, *New York: A Guide to the Empire State*, hypes the myth of public bohemia in 1940s Greenwich Village, but then issues a wry warning: "visited by the curious, it listens to a crapulent poet melodramatically reciting his effusions".

James Byrne's second collection is *Blood/Sugar* (Arc). His anthology *Voice Recogntion*, co-edited with Clare Pollard, is published by Bloodaxe.

THE GEOFFREY DEARMER PRIZE 2009

This prize is given annually for the best *Poetry Review* poem written by a poet who doesn't yet have a book. It's funded through the generosity of the family in honour of the poet Geoffrey Dearmer, who was a Poetry Society member. This year's judge is Glyn Maxwell, whose own poem can be found on pp.8-9, and will be awarded by him at a magazine launch and reading at the British Library on April 7th.

Glyn Maxwell

The winner of this year's Geoffrey Dearmer Prize is 'Visitation' by Maitreyabandhu (*PR 99:3*). This plangent sob of a poem is about the indent that something – 'you' – makes upon the speaker's consciousness. The shape of that indent defines, or forlornly seeks to define, what exactly has visited. I don't know what has; I don't know what *you* is. None of this vagueness is a problem for me: it is extremely hard to capture this kind of sensation. The humble and provisional phrasing – "that you should come / like that", "in the mess of things", "But even that's too bright"– quietly but absolutely persuades us of the presence of a mind steadied and paused by light. At moments like this the mind does not – as ninety-nine in a hundred poets would – spin off into the brilliantly inventive, immobilizing us with metaphor; it inhales and holds, and gently – inadequate simile by slightly less inadequate simile – builds a case for this experience in the language until language has done its utmost. How honest and deft it is to ponder greyness for a whole stanza and then, having confidently bestrode the stanza-break, to settle – a bit aghast – for saying: "Grey". To quote the poet, most poetry is too 'world-we're-busy-in': here is a brief encounter with the ineffable, and a reminder that poetry is more honoured by sounding the limits of language than by pretending there are none.

Also commended are Jeri Onitskansky for 'The Distinct' and Fani Papageorgiou for 'Caramel'.

Maitreyabandhu
Visitation

Strange that you should come
like that, without any form at all,
carrying no symbolic implements,
without smile or frown
or any commotion,
as if you had been there all the time,
like a pair of gloves left in a pocket.

As if I had been looking that way,
into the wide blue yonder, and you were
beside me, enduring my hard luck stories
with infinite patience. Not even waiting –
the tree outside my window
doesn't wait, nor the ocean-wedge
with its new, precise horizon – just there
like the shadow of a church

or a quiet brother.
And how I saw you, in the mess of things,
was as a slant of grey,
the perfect grey of house dust,
an absolute neutral, with no weaving,
no shimmer of cobalt
and light-years away from Byzantium.

Grey. And I want to add, like light,
as if a skylight opened in my skull,
and into the darkness fell
a diagonal of pure Bodmin Moor.
But even that's too bright,
too world-we're-busy-in.
Call it 'dust' then, or the bloom
of leaf-smoke from an autumn fire.

SAVE 50% ON A TLS SUBSCRIPTION

For people who want the best coverage of literature, culture and the arts, with incisive, informed and truly original reviews and debate, The Times Literary Supplement is the perfect publication. Buy a subscription from only £16.75 a quarter and we'll also send you a free TLS book bag.

TLS

FOR LOVERS OF LITERARY CULTURE

"The TLS has competitors and even enemies, but no rivals. Everyone is happy to acknowledge its influence, its fame and its authority" – LE MONDE

TO SAVE 50% CALL 01858 438 781
QUOTING S107 OR VISIT
WWW.SUBSCRIPTION.CO.UK/TLS/S107
and have the TLS delivered direct to your door every week.